Designer
&Client

Designer &Client

Eight Boat Design Commissions, from Kayak to Cruiser

BY ANTONIO DIAS

A WoodenBoat Book

Book and Cover Design: Lindy Gifford
Printed in the U.S.A.

Published by WoodenBoat Publications
PO Box 78, Naskeag Road
Brooklin, Maine 04616 USA

ISBN 0-937822-51-5

TO THE MEMORY OF CASIMIRO PIRES DIAS
2/2/01 - 2/27/75

My father was born at the time of the death of Queen Victoria and died after Watergate. Through the stories he retold around the dinner table in my youth, I have had accounts of Halley's Comet, the sinking of the *Titanic*, and the first day of school for a Brazilian youngster newly arrived in Lisbon in 1910.

He was 51 when I was born, and his experiences 30 or 40 years before that were my first introductions to a longer time scale than the future-crazed 1950s otherwise allowed me. If his memory extended back half a century, now reaching close to a full one, then it was easier to imagine that history was actually lived by people—and was not just a litany of dates in a textbook.

My father's father had owned lumber warehouses in Sao Paulo, Brazil, and in Portugal. Many times I've imagined what those stacks of giant boles of mahogany or chestnut must have been like. The smell of shavings or sawdust can still bring that imagined memory to mind.

My father died while I was still in "boat school." The price for having his long view into the past was that I could only carry him forward in my memory. It's to that memory that I dedicate this book.

ACKNOWLEDGEMENTS

No matter how many have come along a similar path before, our own journey inevitably strikes us as something unique and filled with import. Having glanced through so many other authors' acknowledgments lists, I now find myself in the same place and realize the need to mention and thank sincerely all those who've helped me. At the same time, I recognize the fleeting interest this generates for most readers.

I've always been one to stay for the credits at the movies, and while most people do flee at the sight of "The End" so as not to miss the traffic jam in the parking lot, some of us do stay behind to note the names of those involved in creating what we've just enjoyed. Books are a bit different; the acknowledgments go at the beginning, and there is no rush at the door to avoid them. Still it's not just the names on the poster that brought the work to completion; the contributions others have made warrants mention. I trust that a few of you readers feel the same way and are interested to know.

I first want to thank my collaborators—notably Jenny Bennett, Peter Chesworth, John and Dee Deegan, Jeff Halpern, Mike O'Brien, Bill Page, Peter H. Spectre, and Gordon and Doris Swift—for all they've done to flesh out the premise of this book. I've been very lucky to be able to work with such fine people.

Peter H. Spectre and Kathleen Brandes have also been indispensable in getting me through the many phases of turning an idea into a bound work. Lindy Gifford, the book's designer, has taken a pile of drawings and disks and wrought it all into a unified whole—a particularly challenging task in light of the preponderance of illustrations and the stubbornness of my own ideas on the matter.

Carl Cramer, the publisher at WoodenBoat, has been a friend and adviser for years; his agreement that my hunch was worth following up came at the very start of this project. Jim Miller has seen to it that all of the fiscal realities, so far from my own competence, have been taken care of.

Without drawing this out to include a whole genealogy of precedents and helpful souls, I must mention a few without whose help I could never have reached this point. First comes Ernest ("Ernie") Brierley, my onetime teacher at the Washington County Vocational Technical Institute in Lubec, Maine. He was my first teacher of boatbuilding and design. I still have ship's curves "borrowed" from his set that I use every day, symbols of everything else I have from him in my head. I did have the opportunity to see him not long before his death, and I hope I was able to give him a sense of the gratitude that I've developed for him over the years.

I want to thank my "lucky stars" to have had the opportunity to spend two years at WCVTI in the early 1970s. It was the kind of messy, "inefficient" learning environment that gives one the chance to learn how to learn—and not just passively accept a transfusion of predigested "content."

Now it gets personal—it always does. Give the soldier a chance in front of a microphone and he'll invariably say, "Hi, Mom!" To my parents I owe so much—don't we all? For starters, and apropos of the subject at hand, they gave me the chance to grow up on that beach on Cape Cod. It was a singular upbringing that has convinced me that singular upbringings are the only ones worth giving a child.

Finally, I want to thank my wife, Katherine Mehls. Two incredible events—if I may lift them out of the myriad choices made and paths taken in this life—have shaped my life more profoundly than all others. The first was my parents' decision to settle in Truro, Massachusetts, instead of Newark, New Jersey, before I was born. The second was my whim to go to a friend's birthday party, where I met Kay.

CONTENTS

INTRODUCTION

I came to boatbuilding and boat design in the early 1970s, near the beginning of the resurgence of interest in traditional boats—a period of transition. The traditions of wooden boatbuilding and boat and yacht design had just about come to an end, and a few people were getting together, trying to keep them from disappearing without a trace.

The boats themselves were the most appealing aspect of a past that had all but vanished: No Man's Land boats, Kingston lobsterboats, peapods, dories—a heritage in working craft that men such as Howard Chapelle had documented over the preceding 30 years. These weren't the ships that a museum might take on, but small craft that had been without champions. Many of us wanted to build these boats, either for ourselves or for the buyers we were convinced would appear once they saw what we saw....

But it wasn't that simple. Some of us did build our boats, or restored old ones. A few builders were able to scrape by with a trickle of buyers. The "revolution" didn't come.

Actually, just when it seemed to be arriving, it appeared to be taking a 180-degree turn from where we had hoped. The "market" for dories, Whitehalls, etc., never did materialize. Traditional ways had lost their grip on how Americans lived.

To my benefit, I was able to follow my proclivities instead of my father's footsteps, as tradition might have dictated. But there was a trade-off. The integrated entry into the field I had chosen was there no longer. Without an apprenticeship—a step-by-step, incremental growth of experience leading toward a known goal—it was necessary for us who chose this route to blunder through, following our instincts and inclinations as best we could, hoping to arrive somewhere, somehow.

There's a certain irony in turning to a nonconformist path in a desire to follow tradition. It's often stated that if Nathanael Herreshoff or John Alden were alive today, they would be building fiberglass boats. Whether or not that's true, chances are they wouldn't be far from the mainstream. The pursuit of their traditions was left to dreamers and artists more interested in capturing a feeling, an ethos, than winning a race or chasing efficiency.

Over the years, it became apparent that slavish imitation wouldn't do, either. The boats we admired were tied to their times; we are tied to ours. If a connection were possible, it would have to be through an act of translation. To try to bridge this perceived gap, I've studied the way traditional craft were conceived, and the reasons why certain choices apparently were made. I've hoped to bring this experience to bear, creating boats that are functional yet still embody the counterbalancing values that have appealed to me since my youth.

It's hard to make use of the highly charged term *values* these days when the only meaning ascribed to the word with any unanimity is financial. Too rarely is the possibility considered that values could relate to a positive nostalgia—looking to the past for solace or redemption, not merely as a marketing ploy. It is seen only as uncritical escapism distracting us from "progress."

It may seem ludicrous to expect boats—and pleasure boats at that—to be vehicles for a search for truth. Aren't they toys, conspicuous consumption, status symbols? How could they be anything else? Twenty-odd years down this path, I must say that I still have reason to doubt this conventional wisdom. I continue to see glimmers of the transformative powers inherent in boats and refuse to abandon my expectations.

So much of what we do is, or seems to be, required of us. We manage to develop plenty of excuses for blaming our choices on necessity. The scope for free choice seems to narrow every year, and youngsters "buy into it" almost as soon as they can walk. Hurtling along the determined path faster and faster, there are fewer chances to question any of it. It's easy to put owning a boat near the top of the conspicuous consumer's shopping list—just treat it as another part of the earn-and-spend cycle. No, I don't think it has to be that way.

If we can back off a bit (an effort in itself), we can see that no one is forcing us to have a pleasure boat. No practical purpose is fulfilled by owning one, so the necessity simply does not exist. What's left? Free choice.

A boat is an opportunity to create a dream and act on it. Most such dreams are modest: to float..., to be in the outdoors..., to escape distractions. The sacrifice involved, however, is relatively great, the cost in money and time almost always just beyond reach. Yet many of us seem to live for this. Why? Finding answers to that question is fundamental to designing boats. There may be as many answers as questioners, but I think they all have to do with the tensions between freedom and security, risk and relaxation that we find in boats.

A boat demands investment from us. And I don't just mean financial investment. Every boat presents a challenge; that's what makes it seem almost alive. Without care, boats die—and a dying or dead boat is, at the very least, heart-wrenching. The more time we give to boats, the more they thrive—and the strange part is, so do we. They open us to their own rhythms and to those of the waters they carry us over and through. For many of us, there was a first, vivid experience of the magic cast by a boat.

I grew up on a beach, literally, and one of my earliest memories is of being handed over the transom of a daysailer from that Cape Cod shore. The water was perfectly still (that's why I was being entrusted to the boat that day), and the only air was offshore. Not a ripple marred the perfectly transparent surface of the water. As my weight came down into the boat, the boat pushed back—a dynamic, not static, equilibrium. My sensation was not of flying—I was floating. No other word describes the feeling, and, laughably simple as it may seem, I think many of us have squandered fortunes trying to repeat that sensation.

As contact with the shore was broken that day, the boat started to glide away from the land and I could see the bottom—but no surprises there. Even at that toddler stage, I'd spent many hours walking on the sand at low tide now below the boat's keel. This, though, was different. The water acted as a lens, magnifying the pebbles and shells and tinting them brilliantly. I seemed to climb higher and higher above the sand while traveling outward perfectly level—sea level, in fact.

I don't remember now who put me in that boat, although I remember the grip under my arms and the pressure of a life vest under my chin. It was someone I trusted; I didn't resist. I was open to the wonders laid before me that day. I know I ultimately have my parents to thank for giving me that chance, and it was probably one of them who handed me in. It's amazing, after all parents go through, to realize how offhand some of the greatest gifts they bestow on their children can seem at the time.

That one moment some 40 years ago—not more than 60 seconds of impressions—has had a lasting impact on my aspirations, my dreams, my life. It was a baptism of sorts, an introduction to all of the variables I now try to confront with vellum and pen, hard disk and mouse. It was all there in that moment.

I guess I'm bringing up that old story to bump into a number of important points. It pinpoints a crucial moment that led me, eventually, to design. It shows the way the simplest contact with boats can be a transforming experience in one's life, and the precious quality of time on the water. It describes an enduring gift parents can give their children, when too few gifts are truly memorable—try as we might to make them so.

The adult in my story was the person who introduced me to the boating experience. Most simply put, it could be to fill that adult role that I design boats. This is the way I can put other people into boats—give them something of what I received that day. Of course, it's not that simple—neither the explanation nor the doing. When it comes down to it, though, it's this process, in eight variations, that forms the basis of this book.

———————————

As part of my self-guided "apprenticeship" over the past decade or so, I have developed the habit of asking knowledgeable and interested people to give me parameters for the boat they'd "like" to have—regardless of time and money and other extenuating factors. I value the opportunity to bring in fresh viewpoints to stimulate my thinking, and I've found this a worthwhile exercise. After doing this for a time, I began to collect these "commissions." When I met retired boatbuilder/yacht broker Bill Page some years back, he expressed interest in the cartoon of one of the designs in my catalog, and we began to correspond about ways we could alter the design. As time went on, we developed that cartoon into the boat shown in this book as *Southern Waters*. Without realizing it, we had also started down the path to the creation of this book.

After Bill came Peter Chesworth, the English marine photographer who's worked for *Classic Boat*, *The Boatman*, and now *Water Craft* magazines. I also invited Jenny Bennett, who's been an editor for *Classic Boat*, *The Boatman*, and *WoodenBoat*, to commission a design.

What had begun as an impulse to generate ideas evolved into a series of designs for people I respect in the field. Then came the idea to formalize and expand the group and create this book. The others were asked as they showed interest, and a range and balance of designs evolved.

The project was meant to serve two purposes. First, it gave me valuable input from people I admire and respect. Second, it was also an opportunity to illustrate my design philosophy with a variety of intriguing examples. These designs have been a challenge to produce. Documenting them—and explaining how they came to be—made this even more of a challenge. The boating-world professionals who shared their expertise and enthusiasm—thus providing the shape for this book of designs—stand out in rather remarkable contrast to what I see as a fundamental change, over the last few decades, in the relationship between boat client and boat designer.

———————

There was a time when everyone involved knew his or her role in a fairly standard script. People with boats had had them for generations—either as watermen and fishermen or as wealthy yacht owners or well-to-do professionals. They all lived in waterfront communities and were immersed in the maritime culture.

Today that system has broken down, in part because of the new profile of the typical boat buyer. The heirs of those who made up the old market, living in boating communities, have enjoyed an unbroken tradition—but most buyers now come from outside this group. Many people are new to boating, others live far from traditional centers. Their backgrounds often equip them poorly to meet the challenges involved in commissioning a new boat. With absolutely no prior experience, many are even looking for a boat they can build themselves. (Sometimes, miraculously, it works; many times, disaster results.)

Traditional boats have become submerged in an enormous, consumer-driven mass market in marine products, and the boating press, with a few exceptions, is propelled by this mass market. Anyone looking for a way past all that—looking for something different—is in for a difficult time trying to sort it all out.

One problem with the sorting-out process can be summed up by a friend's quip, "Lie to me—everyone else does." We have grown accustomed to being lied to, and to liking it. In this ad-driven age, almost every form of public speech patronizes the listener. Everything is couched in a language of ease. All problems will disappear miraculously if you buy what is being sold. "Be cool." "Take it easy." "No sweat." I'm afraid these attitudes don't have much to do with what it takes to have a boat.

As a designer, I have to tell clients and potential clients some uncomfortable truths. A boat costs money and demands a lot of time. Owning a boat is far more complicated than applying for a new credit card. Naturally, we hope that all the effort will end up being worthwhile, but for that to happen, it's crucial to face the issues squarely.

———————

Having a custom boat designed or built is not the same as purchasing a large consumer item, such as a car. The wary cynicism we bring to "shopping" for a car or a washing machine isn't the best trait to nurture for the relationships needed to have a boat designed and built. These relationships have to be personal, not based on mistrust or standoffishness—and they can be intense. While most of us crave authentic interactions—one-on-one experiences—we usually lack a track record with them.

Trust between designer and client is essential. If you are planning to own a boat, you will need to put your private hopes and desires, as well as significant financial resources, into the hands of strangers. This shouldn't be done lightly, and every effort must be made to ensure that your trust is well placed. At that point, though, it is essential to put faith in the relationship and remain open to the results.

A major aspect of trust is having confidence in your choice of designer, and nowadays there is a bewildering array of people designing boats. Some have degrees in naval architecture or marine engineering; others have gained their experience through less formal yet equally reliable means. There is talk of standardizing the profession with licensing and other bureaucratic trappings, but I don't think they will solve anything except the bureaucrat's need to categorize and supervise.

Ask around. Read. Look for a designer whose previous work most closely fits your sensibility, and one you can talk to. (Disappointing outcomes often result from poor communication.) Get a sense of the designer's reputation within the boating community. Then make your choice.

Once you have made a decision, keep in mind that you are paying for the designer's experience (as well as that of the builder you eventually choose), so be willing and prepared to get your money's worth. Accepting the results of experts' advice, even when it may be hard to take, is the only way to take full advantage of the services rendered. All that may sound obvious—and, needless to say, it hasn't been much of an issue for the commissions in this book—but such ideal collaboration in fact is rare. As a result, many people unfortunately squander the opportunity to which their expenditure entitles them.

I realize I may risk sounding like a Svengali, trying to lure victims into my domain, but I feel it's crucial to urge clients not to be timid or reluctant to explore their own ideas along with the possibilities suggested by the designer. The spouse of one client characterized me as "the devil"—not in a malicious sense, but by way of explaining that I'm always urging people to give form to their desires.

It's easy to feel trapped in a certain idea of what our boat "must" be; we lose track of the fact that there is no "must." We can choose what we want, and alter that choice if necessity impinges. If the first idea proves impractical, we can alter our expectations in ways that restore the balance between what we want and what we can afford.

The obvious case is that of settling for a smaller boat than originally envisioned. Too often, this decision is made to save money, with little regard for the changes wrought on the boat's suitability for the chosen purpose. Unless the smaller craft's mission is adjusted and we understand the implications, this option can be a mistake. Instead of being a simple trade-off of size versus cost, the whole issue must be explored with the designer, who will help sort out which aspects of the dream need to be modified and what modifications need to be made.

Limits chosen of our free will, for the pursuit of joy, cease to be the burdens of necessity and become part of a game. Designer/builder/author Pete Culler said, "Experience starts when you begin." I'd like to add, "The fun starts when you begin." That is, the entire process, from the first wish to the last sail, is a game freely chosen. It is played to your own "rules." Enjoy the process.

The whole process, in fact—from inspiration to first sail and beyond—should be a wonderful adventure, not a chore to be gotten past. I don't know how to stress this point enough. People too often erect a "starting line" across their paths. It falls sometime in the future, when a certain condition has been met: the laying of the keel, the launching, the first sail. Only after that point has been reached, they vow, can they start enjoying the boat. Often they never reach that moment, or even if they do, they have become so accustomed to postponing their joy that it never seems to arrive. In today's lingo, "Go for it."

The thought of embarking on a custom design scares many of the people I meet at boat shows or through correspondence. The idea is even intimidating for those who want to build their own boat and sail away. Even if they have spent years looking for a boat and are dissatisfied with what they've found, many won't look beyond a "stock" design. While stock plans have their place, I'm afraid the ill-considered jump to choose one is a common mistake.

What is a stock design? When a designer has developed a boat for someone, the client has bought permission to build one boat, but he doesn't own the design. The designer is free to sell copies of the plans, often at a deep discount from what the original client paid. At first blush, this seems to be a "no-brainer." Let someone else pay for the work, then show up and buy the stock plan.

Why should someone looking for a new wooden boat not automatically assume that a stock plan is the best route? The reasons go back to the differences in our circumstances from those of 50 years ago. Then, almost all boats were custom built, even those built from stock designs. The wooden construction methods made each boat unique, easily adaptable to the owner's needs. Experienced builders worked in the custom details, so the hunger for individuality wasn't as hard to satisfy as it is today.

Most prospective boat owners, if asked, will say they haven't even considered talking to a designer. If only the wealthy can afford a custom house, they assume it must be doubly true of a custom boat. As they embark on what already seems an extravagant path toward boat ownership, hiring a designer appears a foolhardy shortcut to bankruptcy. For those intending to build their own boat, a spirit of do-it-yourself self-sufficiency takes hold, and choosing a design is part of that challenge. There's also our natural reluctance to pay for something intangible. Spending good money on paper seems a waste, when the whole boat still has to be paid for.

Sadly, many people today feel that spending about 10 percent of the boat's cost on design work is not an affordable expenditure. My feeling is that clients on a budget, but committed to building a boat, will benefit enormously from the cooperation of a designer. By making the investment in design, and in the counsel of a designer, they can protect the investment they are making.

The most common reason for dissatisfaction with or abandonment of a boat project results from inaccurately predicting the needs and usage expected of the boat. Saving the design fee will not let you build a schooner instead of a dory, but the assistance of a designer may save you from having built a schooner when you would have been satisfied with a dory.

But with so many classic designs available at low cost, why bother with a living designer? Well, there are good reasons. Recently, I had a series of conversations with a man eight years into building a large schooner to a classic design. He was thinking about making some modifications. As we got deeper into our discussion, it became clear that some equipment choices he'd already made were potentially detrimental to the boat's handling, and perhaps even her ultimate seaworthiness. How had this happened?

The designer of that schooner has been dead for many years, and his plans had been left vague regarding some elements that this amateur builder decided to change. In the era when the plans were drawn, designers always assumed their boats would be built by experienced yards. Over the years, equipment considered standard has changed, and now a novice amateur builder had taken on an ambitious solo project, far from experienced help. Short of a seance, he would never know what the designer would have done to solve his present dilemma. The lack of an ongoing dialogue with the designer, before choosing the design as well as during construction, has cost him time, money, and peace of mind. This combination leads many amateurs to grief.

I find that the deeper I draw from traditional craft, the more I see my job as one of interpretation, even translation, of designs of the past. I attempt to fit their desirable aspects into today's vernacular, to strike a balance between the traits that attract us and the demands these craft must meet today.

We tend to think anachronism applies only to things. An engine in a peapod strikes us the way a boombox on a blacksmith's workbench would. Yet, when we attempt to inhabit something old, we forget that we have become the anachronisms. Dressed in period costume (though few of us would go that far), we would still retain the expectations and mental habits of our time. It can be a rude awakening to discover how limited is our tolerance for the conditions of 1890, or even 1950. What holds our fascination is a small portion of the totality these artifacts contain. It's only through a process of translation that we can enjoy them and fit them into our lives, instead of being frustrated by them.

If my view has any validity, then few if any of us can fill the shoes of the typical early reader of William Atkin's *Book of Boats*. These men (and almost all were male) could fit the "salty" products of that designer's office directly into their lives. The assumptions were shared, the materials well known to all, the expected usage well understood. Today, without a guide or a translator to adapt these types to contemporary conditions, the typical person attracted to those boats would have difficulty fitting them into his or her life.

If the search for the unique underlies the pursuit, why begin with a boat designed for someone else? This seems so obvious as to need no discussion, yet few people follow through on this insight. There are no perfect boats. There may be good combinations: a good boat well suited to the owner's expectations. Every boat was designed for a particular circumstance, at a particular time, for a particular person. The boat best suited to your circumstances, your time, and your personality is most likely to be one designed specifically for you.

Our circumstances eventually boil down to financial resources, so one of the most essential requirements for a custom project is a realistic budget. We tend to have a vague notion that boats are expensive but seem reluctant to examine how much they really cost. Often the designer's proposed fee and first rough estimate of overall cost are the first hard evidence people face in this regard. Inflation—a monster seemingly vanquished by our current crop of financial leaders—has, over the years, played havoc with our sense of what a boat should cost. Those of us more steeped in old cruising yarns than today's price structures are more familiar with costs 30 or 40 years old.

A few years ago, there was a controversy in the letters column of *WoodenBoat* magazine over the rumored cost of a new Rozinante. A classic case. On the one hand, as readers of L. Francis Herreshoff's *Sensible Cruising Designs* know, L. Francis rationalized the omission of a companionway slide to save a few hundred dollars. But we tend to forget that when he wrote those words in the 1950s, a Buick cost less than $2,000. Now it's closer to $30,000. I'm afraid that companionway slide may cost as much now as the whole boat did in the 1950s.

Get past the notion that there are "sharp operators" making a "killing" in the design or construction of small wooden boats. There are greener pastures elsewhere for that type of operation. The notion that "efficiency" would somehow keep prices at some arbitrary low level is exaggerated. The differences between the least efficient and the most efficient builder's cost may be 10 percent, certainly not enough to restore those thrilling prices of yesteryear.

I am no financial adviser; my advice begins with the sum you have allocated. Nevertheless, I feel many people could afford more boat if they carefully scrutinized spending habits and prioritized their discretionary spending. Money spent on momentary distractions, out of a sense of frustration, can add up considerably. If your budget is really too small to deal with the realities of a newly built boat, all is not lost. The used-boat market, especially the one for interesting vintage boats, is quite low, and it's possible to find boats for as little as 20 percent of their build cost. With the "major" boat out of the way, there might be enough left in the pot to exercise one's creativity on a small boat done new.

There are two broad categories of older wooden boats on the market: those needing a major refit and those that recently had one. The best bargains are in the second category—if you're after a boat to use right away. One needing extensive work will have a lower price, but unless you plan to do the work yourself, and treat that time as recreation (there are worse ways to spend your time), it will cost more in the long run. Remember that most refitted boats do not recoup the added investment if resold over the short term.

The "project boat," needing significant work, may make sense as a halfway step between a restored boat and a custom-built boat. It can give you the chance to fit the boat to your needs and give you a strong sense of having created the boat yourself. The problem is that it can be difficult to keep the cost sufficiently lower than new work to justify the effort. The desire to restore a boat for the enjoyment of owning a classic vessel must be weighed against the advantages of starting with a clean slate.

It's essential to consult an experienced surveyor when considering a used boat. If a major restoration is to be attempted, whether do-it-yourself or by a professional boatbuilder, consult a designer as well. Just as with a new custom design for a "traditional" boat, the restoration will be a translation of the boat's earlier self, and a similar analysis is valuable.

As with all strategies for boat ownership, there are no "steals" in the older-boat market. A prudent use of the available budget requires careful consideration. There's nothing wrong, per se, with having an unrequited dream of boat ownership—a dream fed with doses of blueprints. Armchair sailing. I've done a great deal of that myself, and I find it satisfying. While this habit can be maintained modestly on a diet of books and catalogs with a few study plans stirred into the mix, armchair sailing can go wrong.

I see people whose dream has grown by fits and starts without a consistent plan or overview. They've salted away hardware, gathered a stash of white oak, and amassed a stack of bargain plans. What's missing is a realistic assessment of the final cost of consummating the project, and of how these arbitrary elements can ever add up. While a dreamer may choose this route in an attempt to save money, it may end up costing more than a well-planned campaign and result in the death of the dream as well.

I don't know the true ratio of lost dreams to actual boats built. Probably no one does. From my own observations and those of friends and associates, I suspect it is extraordinarily high. This obstacle seems to sink more boats than any physical reef or hazard, but it should not lead us to despair. Boating people welcome a certain level of risk if it can be faced with some planning and forethought. This should be the case here, as well.

———————

I hope this discussion of the financial side of boat design will help you avoid some of the potential pitfalls. The whole story of custom boat design essentially comes down to seeking good advice and following it; looking for a relationship with good rapport and developing it. Most important, it means getting past the notion that enjoyment of a boat starts with the first sail. It can and should start with the first discussion of her possible configuration, continue through an enlightening design stage and interesting construction, and culminate in enjoyable boating.

It may be futile trying to explain pitfalls to the enthusiast in advance, because one tends to rush past such advice on the way to the "good stuff." Experience seems to show that such warnings tend to remain unheeded until the first rush of enthusiasm has been blunted on

Designer & Client a bit of adversity. I suppose the wish to impart advice and caveats comes from the same source as the urge to design. One sees things in need of correction and sets out to use understanding as a tool to make those changes. Forgive my zealotry.

In the chapters that follow, I hope to show the way a handful of experienced boaters with differing points of view can illuminate a range of the possible outcomes for design commissions. Perhaps you'll even recognize a bit of yourself in some of these accounts.

CHAPTER I

Small

Jenny Bennett was instrumental in turning my vague notions into a book of designs. Creating a design for her was a catalyst for this project, and she became a valuable sounding board for me when I started to develop the idea further.

Jenny is most familiar to North American readers from her recent stint as an editor at *WoodenBoat* magazine, but she has had a long career in boating periodicals that belies her age. She spent her childhood sailing and teaching sailing in her native Devon, England. Along with Peter Chesworth (see next chapter) and Pete Greenfield, Jenny was involved in the startup of *Classic Boat* magazine, and all three were responsible for *The Boatman* magazine as well.

She writes about boats out of a passionate commitment to her subject, and there is a warmth to her pieces often lacking when technical details are left to fend for themselves. Her stories may take unexpected turns, but there's always a sense of being in good hands as you follow her train of thought.

We met in March 1995 at the Maine Boatbuilders' Show in Portland, where I've made many significant contacts over the years. Our next encounter was at the WoodenBoat Show in Southwest Harbor that June, when I offered to design a boat for her. We share a fascination with New England fishing schooners, and there were some great examples at the show to whet our appetites. We tentatively decided to work up a 45-foot schooner, but on further reflection, Jenny came to the conclusion that while she has always admired the big American schooners, the chances of her ever being in a position to own one were too slim. She preferred a boat type that has been part of her life all along, the British dayboat. Here was a boat she could actually plan to build. So in short order Jenny sent me a list of first impressions of what she was looking for:

> Good sailing performance, fast but not exhausting, heeling enough to require a bit of effort but not so that you capsize. *Small* enough for singlehanded sailing, large enough for two adults to sail together with a whole bundle of camping gear-i.e., two sleeping bags, one tent, two gear bags.
>
> Either open or with a foredeck (if open, must have means for fitting some kind of waterproof tarp across from gunwale to gunwale). *Simple* but good-looking and efficient rig: maybe gunter, maybe high-peaked gaff, maybe standing lug, probably two sails.
>
> And here they come, the four crunch things:
>
> Has to be pretty and probably have an air of traditional. Must be light enough and flat enough for me to drag up a gently sloping sandy beach or for two to carry/drag up a steeper beach (this for camping). Must row well for when the wind dies. And everything, but everything, must have a stowage place (even if it's just clips on the centerboard case) so that when you're sailing, you're not constantly shoving errant oars, paddles, etc., out from under your feet.
>
> P.S.: I like a bit of sheer.

Harry

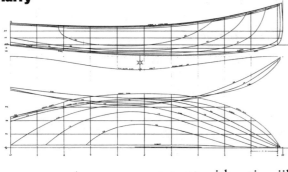

Jenny and I had gone out in my sailing dinghy, *Harry*. Designed for my own use, *Harry* is 14 feet long, glued lapstrake, and has a high-peaked gaff cat rig with a jib on a bowsprit. I based the design on a combination of the features of a 10-foot Penn Yan sailing dinghy I'd sailed in Lubec, Maine, 20 years ago, and Uffa Fox's early International 14s. The rig, like that of the Penn Yan, started out as a cat with a tiny jib set to the stemhead. It is surprising how much is gained by a jib of 10 square feet. The performance was significantly better with the "slot" effect of this sail, over a mainsail alone.

Harry is fast and very stiff. One thing led to another, as is often the case when a designer has free reign to tinker. I added a bowsprit and cut down an old jib from a Windmill. It sets from a traveler ring on the bowsprit and can be brought inboard for ease of handing. *Harry* has been a lot of fun, and so far there are two sisterships.

Jenny's boat provided a chance to carry out some of the lessons learned with *Harry*. My one biggest complaint with the Little Cats— as I named that class—was excessive complication of the rig. It helped me exorcise some of my frustration at not having a big boat, but it did make setting up off the trailer much more complicated than necessary. I also felt that a "de-tuned" version of the boat—one with a bit more freeboard and a smaller, more manageable sail plan—would make a better all-around daysailer.

Later that winter, Jenny called me with some further thoughts on the new boat. When thinking about this new concept, she kept in mind English designer Andrew Wolstenholme's Mallard design for *The Boatman* magazine. Jenny had been editor when it was designed, but the commission had not been geared to her personal requirements. She wanted this boat to be "hers."

The traditional British dayboat goes back at least to the time of Captain Bligh and his 1,000-mile plus journey in a ship's boat—after he'd landed (so to speak) in a bit of difficulty with certain members of his crew. The conditions on England's shores are strenuous compared to most American waters, and a small, open boat must be capable of handling rough water even in bays and estuaries. As a result, British dinghies tend to be substantial boats. Construction has been lap-strake—clinker, as they call it—with heavy scantlings. A 12-footer might weigh 300 or 400 pounds and have a miniature cutter rig with roving bowsprit, and sometimes even a topsail. The boats may be heavy and slow, but they are sure—and ready for anything.

Using glued lap construction, it's possible to make a much lighter variant of the traditional dayboat—one capable of handling the trials of life on a trailer while maintaining the earlier boat's capabilities. Conventional planking, whether lapstrake or carvel, isn't well suited to the extreme conditions encountered by a boat on a trailer. Of the two, lapstrake is better able to handle the drying effects of blasting down the highway than carvel, but the shocks of an uneven road can still shake things apart. Glued lap construction cannot dry out, and it's monocoque—all one piece.

Jenny thought 13 feet would be an ideal length—short enough for easy trailering and light enough to be run up the beach by hand; long enough to take out a group of friends and have a decent turn of speed. She reiterated the need for simplicity, in fittings and rig. Whether a high-peaked gaff or a standing lug rig, the spars and sails should all stow in one bag, and if there were a bowsprit, it should be easily removable. The point of all this is to streamline the setup time to no more than 10 or 15 minutes. Related to the need for simplicity, she wanted each piece of gear to have its own storage spot. The rudder and tiller, for instance, should have brackets to hold them against the centerboard case for trailering. The oars should fit under the seats.

Jenny plans to go on camp cruises of up to two weeks, so stowage space and convenient accommodation for two in sleeping bags are essential. Because of the need for storage, no permanent flotation tanks were requested. On cruises, watertight bags filled with clothing and gear will be lashed in to provide buoyancy. Otherwise, inflatable buoyancy bags can do the job.

I suggested the centerboard case be placed off-center. This has been done on a number of American beach boats, most notably the No Man's Land boats. Keel construction thus is stronger and simpler: a narrow vertical member, not the flat and tapered keel of the usual centerboarder. It also helps protect the slot and board from abrasion and makes it less likely to jam with pebbles or shell. Since the case is set beside the keel in one of the garboards at the rabbet, it isn't in full contact with the beach.

Preliminary cartoon

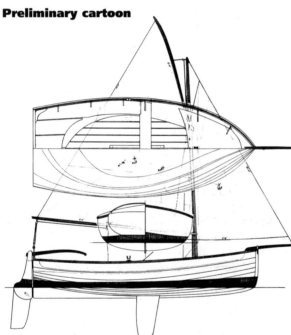

Jenny wanted a foredeck. The dayboats she knew had a deck at the level of the thwarts instead of up at the sheer. This makes it easier to go forward, or to go over the bow onto the beach, without having to perch atop the bow on a high, narrow foredeck. What works at a larger size loses practicality at this scale.

In keeping with the need to beach easily, the rudder will have a drop blade. I've found with *Harry* that the combination of a foil cross section for the centerboard and a high-aspect drop blade on the rudder helps a gaff-headed boat point well.

There will be two sets of reef points, and the halyards will belay to pins in the mast thwart. The main is rigged with a downhaul. It sets loose-footed on a boom with a bronze traveler across the transom. As I discovered with *Harry,* the sail needs a high peak, another secret to a gaff rig with good windward ability.

Jenny also wanted the boat to be stable enough to live on a mooring, so that she wouldn't "have to work too hard to keep it upright." At the same time, she was after speed as well as stability: "At the Wednesday evening races, I don't want to be at the back of the pack."

The following March, I gave her the first draft of the design. Later, after she had studied what I had done, she sent the blueprint back with her notes and changes, the most obvious of which were to the rig. The bowsprit was eliminated, and the sail plan was increased in height to compensate. She roughed in the wineglass transom I had neglected.

In an early draft of any design, I'm more concerned with setting an overall tone than in getting every detail the way it was presented to me. It's a good time and place for clients to make their wishes known. By marking up the drawing, they can show me a lot. The changes don't have to make a pretty drawing, or even add up. It's my job to interpret and incorporate them. The clients only need to indicate what they want to see.

I studied Jenny's notes, prepared a revised plan, and sent off the drawings with the following comments:

> I've managed to work up a new draft that I hope will be closer to the mark.
>
> The sail area is a 91 square feet, curved yard, gunter rig. Remember, I have copies of your letters, including your desire to see a curved gaff. I'm not sure how I feel about it. It does keep the sail profile from looking just like a Bermudian sail, for whatever that's worth.

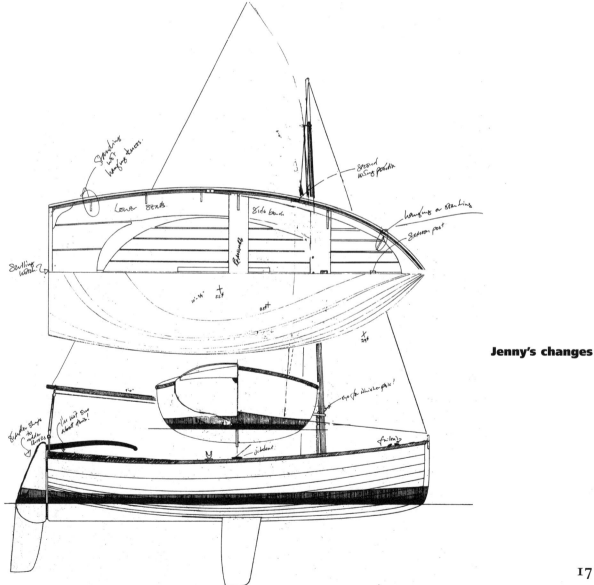

Jenny's changes

The gunter, as opposed to a high-peaked gaff, does save a halyard, in keeping with the theme of simplicity.

How do you feel about a high-peaked standing lug? It can have a similar profile without the added complication of jaws and lacing. It shouldn't interfere with the jib if it's peaked high enough. It would mean abandoning the curved yard, though. My biggest concern with the curved yard is that it may be hard to stow. It complicates the sail bundle.

This hull should be closer to your expectations. Admittedly, the first cartoon was done in a rush in advance of our meeting in Portland. I've narrowed up the stern considerably and lowered the rabbet at the transom, creating the wineglass stern that was lacking. The waterline beam is narrowed to 4 feet 2 inches. The maximum beam has been brought in to 5 feet 4 inches. This will make the boat easier to row while maintaining reserve stability to carry sail.

I estimate the bare boat to weigh about 190 pounds, without the rig or oars aboard. The all-up weight is about 250 pounds. The load waterline shown, at 7¼ inches, is for a displacement of 615 pounds—enough for a crew of two adults, or for you and a lot of camping gear. An added 180 pounds (a third adult) would only sink the boat one more inch.

Rig brought inboard

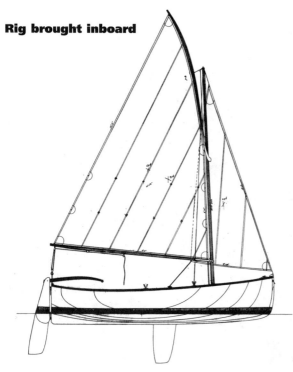

This is a good time for a pause to clarify the term *displacement*, which confuses many people; when applied to small, open boats, it often confuses everybody.

The displacement of a boat isn't its basic weight, as many assume; it's the total weight necessary to sink the boat to the waterline indicated on the plans, the Load Water Line (LWL) or Datum Water Line (DWL). If the boat is intended to float at that depth in use, then the displacement must take into account not only the weight of the boat, but also of the crew and a normal load of gear. Otherwise, the boat will be overloaded with the crew aboard.

The confusion deepens when trying to compare displacement figures for small boats. Out of a desire to shortcut the need to explain all of this in advertising, most commercially available boats list their hull weight as the displacement. This gives a flatteringly low figure but distorts the meaning of the term.

Now, back to my letter to Jenny with my comments on the revised plans:

The sheer has a bit more tuck-up in the stern—the result of lowering the sheer a bit amidships rather than raising it at the transom.

Notice how it wraps around in the perspective views. It saves weight, and it's still high enough to keep out the slop.

The only disagreement I have with your notes is over a samson post. I don't see the need for it. The mast is the strongest mooring post possible without adding complication and weight. I've shown a ring through the stem for a painter. A mooring line tied to the painter will obviate the need for a chock on the rail, and it pulls at a more favorable angle, less likely to depress the bow than a line over the rail.

It may not have been clear on the other drawing, but the knees are standing knees running from the seats and thwarts up to the rail. If the side bench is extended as you suggest, it will be easier to make the center thwart removable. I don't have any problem with lowering the seats. The forward oarlock is where the shrouds attach. There won't be a conflict since it's not possible to row from there without lowering the mast anyway.

Jenny studied the revised plans and then wrote back:

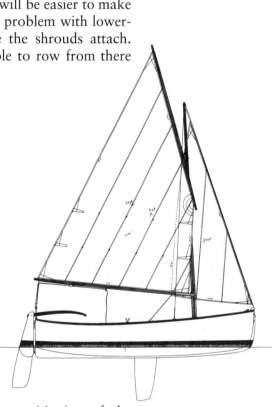

Standing lug variant

> It seems to me that the biggest question mark now (maybe the only question mark) is the rig. I think the way it is at the moment is pretty and will make it look different (always important—who wants exactly what the rest of the crowd has?), but I hear what you say about the curved spar being problematic when it comes to stowing, and I suppose you may well be right. Everything in me says NO to the lug idea because I don't see how it can *not* interfere with the jib. But, if you have time, can you mock up two more sail plans? One gunter with a straight yard, and one for the lug suggestion.
>
> I agree about the samson post, and the positioning of the shrouds; the second rowing position is not a problem. For the rest, I think I'm happy. Is now the moment to say that I'd like any of the mainsail control lines (reef pendants, halyards, etc.) to lead to the starboard side?

I considered Jenny's comments and then came back with more revisions, including a drawing of the new standing-lug rig:

> Enclosed is the long-promised drawing of the standing lug version. I find it the most definitive so far. The curved-yard cartoon seems muddy in comparison. Let me take you through the boat as it stands now.
>
> The interior will be as you requested. The thwarts will have side benches between them. A platform forward creates a storage compartment. Would you prefer it to parallel the sheer or to start just below the sheer at its after end and run horizontally forward, creating higher "bulwarks" at the bow?

Designer & Client

The rail on the Solent gunter drawing is similar to *Harry*'s. It's 3 inches wide and tapered in thickness. It strengthens the hull, keeps spray down, provides a comfortable hiking seat, and creates a deep shadow line on the sheerstrake, accentuating the sheerline and dramatizing its sweep.

This version reminds me of a civilized *Harry*—shorter, less extreme, more wholesome, but with a touch of his elan. The rig is similar to one of the earliest drafts for the Little Cat.

I've shown a downhaul on the main, and a vang. I hope you don't find them too much complication. I think a downhaul rigged back onto the centerboard case simplifies tensioning the luff and allows adjustment while underway for different wind conditions.

Solent Gunter variant

The vang will control sail twist and mitigate the downwind death roll. Remember, you want to be competitive at your Wednesday evening races.

The rig has 91 square feet of sail. This amounts to a sail area/displacement ratio of between 18 and 20 (the range depends on loading). That's plenty of power when you want it. The first reef should tame the rig when you don't. A boat won't go without adequate sail area. Reefing, not undercanvasing, should be the way to deal with stronger winds.

The Solent gunter rig has good sail shape, with short spars and a minimum of hardware. There's a single halyard, simple shrouds run to lashings at the forward rowlock positions. The jib is set flying inside the forestay. It could be hanked on if you prefer. The main has no lacing or hoops or track. On a larger sail, these can cause trouble with the yard on raising or lowering. Once the tension is off the luff, the yard tends to dance around, but this one is small enough to overpower by hand. The gap between the lower luff and the mast puts the leading edge of the sail into cleaner air, away from the mast's wind shadow.

The rudder is pivoting. It doesn't have a lanyard or downhaul. On a boat this size, it's much simpler to have a friction fit and reach back to push the blade down. It will come up on its own if there's an obstruction.

One more point relating to your racing prospects: The foils are shapely and will pay back all the effort you can put into making them as smooth as humanly possible. They merit a surface with a mirror polish. Do that and you'll eat up the other boats to windward. The foils and the bottom should be coated with epoxy and carbon powder. This surface can be sanded very smooth, and is tough and abrasion resistant. Scratches can be filled and sanded back flush without the need to re-coat the whole surface. If you put the boat on a mooring, a hard racing bottom paint will be best. Take the boat to a beach and wipe down the bottom before every race.

The color scheme should be a light color for the topsides. I like ineffable colors, like Harry Green (that's what I call the light gray-green we use on *Harry*), which change with the light conditions. A peach or rose tone will also work well. The boottop should be a strong color or gloss black; the sheerstrake should be bright. The rail can be a strong color, bright red, or a ringing yellow, or brilliant green. The seats are oiled pine, or cedar. The spars are oiled or varnished northern spruce. The sails should be "Egyptian" Dacron.

Let me know how all this strikes you. I would like to await your response before finalizing the interior. The good news is that it should go quickly, since this is a simple boat.

Famous last words. I've found the details for simple little boats can be the hardest to work out. Everything shows, and everything counts aesthetically as well as functionally. Jenny's design was still far from done. In addition, at the time, I was working away learning Minicad, a 3-D computer-assisted-design (CAD) drawing program. This compounded delays on all my projects. The enticement is always the same for computer work: Learn the new program and it will facilitate your work tremendously, speeding up chores and increasing accuracy. In the meantime, everything else is on hold. As time passes, you feel you have a handle on the program's potential; a few days later you discover you hadn't a clue....

In the meantime, Jenny finally chose a name for her boat. She had tried out a couple previously—eventually rejected for one reason or another—and now settled on *Small*, the name of a cherished character in *Winnie the Pooh*, Jenny's childhood favorite—and a name, it turned out, she'd been saving up for some time. In a letter she went into detail on the origin of the name:

> Small is given a whole chapter in *The House at Pooh Corner*, and, since you are one of the uninitiated, here's the most important paragraph:
> "Small's real name was Very Small Beetle, but he was called Small for short, when he was spoken to at all, which hardly ever happened except when somebody said: 'Really, Small.' He had been staying with Christopher Robin for a few seconds, and he started round a gorse-bush for exercise, but instead of coming back the other way, as expected, he hadn't, so nobody knew where he was. 'I expect he's just gone home,' said Christopher Robin to Rabbit. 'Did he say Good-bye-and-thank-you-for-a-nice-time?' said Rabbit. 'He'd only just said how-do-you-do,' said Christopher Robins 'Ha!' said Rabbit. After thinking a little, he went on: 'Has he written a letter saying how much he enjoyed himself, and how sorry he was he had to go so suddenly?' Christopher Robin didn't think he had. 'Ha!' said Rabbit again, and looked very important. "This is Serious. He is Lost. We must begin the Search at once."
> And so everyone in the forest is organized into a search for Small. I think I've always loved the idea that Small, though a very

small creature, was known to be of good character, otherwise no one would have expected him to write a letter to say thank you for his visit. Also, I've always loved that Small, though a very small creature, was worthy of an extensive search that involved everyone even if they didn't know exactly who he was.

Despite the steep learning curve in conquering the CAD program, I fortunately managed to get some work done and sent the results to Jenny.

I thought you might like to see a pair of illustrations I've been working on for *Small*. I've been using Minicad to put together the 3-D model, based on perspective views taken from that program. While learning the program has been frustrating and time-consuming, this is an inkling of the payoff. Along with being able to produce sailing views of a boat that exists only as dancing electrons, I've been able to find storage spaces for oars, tiller, rudder, etc., as you wanted. There will also be full-size patterns for the molds and for the other major structural elements.

The foredeck is flat and set a few inches higher than the side benches and thwart. It rests on a bulkhead just forward of the mast. This bulkhead has an access port into the forepeak on either side of the mast. The foredeck is slatted and gear is stowed in a waterproof sack. An inflatable flotation bag would fit under the deck. The bulkhead is more of a sawn frame with a large opening. If you prefer the deck solid, then there could be small, screw-in hatches. The oars stow under the side benches. The rudder and tiller stow beside the centerboard case.

The boat draws 3 feet with the board down. The high-aspect foil optimizes windward performance with less wetted surface than a triangular-shaped board.

By this time, the seasons had circled around once again. I do believe in spacing out the work on a design over as long a time as possible, so that ideas can percolate and mature, but the design projects detailed in this book took longer than even I would like. This came from my need to intersperse them with more immediately lucrative work and my desire to keep them all going at the same time. I juggled the work to keep everything advancing at roughly parallel speed. Since eight projects are a lot for me to handle at one time, the whole process eventually bogged down. Nevertheless, I managed to finish what I hoped would be the "final" drawings for the lines and sail plan for *Small*, and created a preliminary construction plan. These I gave to Jenny, who took them with her on a visit to her home in Devon, England. She later sent me a letter that said everything that had to be said about her relationship with boats in general, and with *Small* in particular.

Perspective

I can't see any obvious changes that I want on the plan...and the general response at home was, "Ooooohh, sweet little boat." Very gratifying.

In our family album, there's a photograph taken in the summer of 1964. It shows a very young girl clad in shorts, T-shirt, and life jacket, standing on the foredeck of a boat. Given all the relative proportions, you might think the boat quite big, but it is in fact the girl who is small. In 1964, I was two years old. The boat was a 13-foot daysailer called *Wendy Ann*. I don't remember her very clearly, but I know she was the first of a succession of small boats that my parents owned and sailed from their mooring at the bottom of the garden.

One after the other, boats came and went, sold and replaced because they were too small or too large, too tippy or too slow. Some stayed with us for years, becoming well-loved members of the family—*Wendy Ann, Sackbut, Osprey, Kiwi.* Others stayed barely a summer, not even long enough to be named. They were all different, but all had very obvious similarities: They were all wooden, second-hand, and small, open daysailers. Boats were so much a part of my life that I never really thought about them—they just were; an intrinsic part of summer, as accepted and inevitable as homemade lemonade and blackberries in the hedgerows.

My sister, brother, and I joined the local sailing club and raced through the summers in Cadets, Mirrors, Fireflies, Scorpions, Lasers. We joined our peers in the dinghy park and started friendships that have lasted well into adulthood. Other families we knew had yachts, and occasionally I would go away with them for weekends. Such trips were never a great success, as I was invariably seasick, yet I was always anxious for the next invitation.

Perspective

One summer, I asked my mother, "Why don't you buy a yacht?"

Her reply was short and clear: "Because we don't want one."

"But why not?" I persisted.

"Because we don't."

The conversation ended with dissatisfaction on both sides: I was left thinking that it was typical of my mother to explain nothing and that her lack of interest in yacht ownership was just one more example of the incredible stupidity of parents. She, on the other hand, no doubt walked away wondering where this greedy, spoilt child had sprung from, and knowing that any explanation would be wasted on deaf, impatient ears. Now, years later, much the same age as my mother was then, I know exactly why they didn't want a yacht. I know because I don't want one, either.

Maybe I would feel different about it if we had been a yacht-owning family. Instead, I grew up familiar with the presence of a boat always ready and waiting; a boat that you could board and sail away from the mooring in under10 minutes; a boat that was so simple to rig, so easy to use that if you only had half an hour before supper, it was still worth going out; a boat that was small enough that when the wind died and you were up the river half a mile from home, you could drift back with the tide or, at worst, ship the oars and pull your way home.

There was never any pressure involved in my boating—if you felt like going for a sail, you went; if you didn't feel like going, you didn't. But I had, and still have, friends who have to go sailing for the two-week family holiday because the yacht was so expensive to buy, so expensive to moor, so expensive to maintain. It must be used—if only to justify money spent.

"Ah, but," my friends will say, "think of the places we can visit in our yacht, think of the voyages we can make."

But, I will counter, think of the places they can't visit. When, I wonder, did any of them go up the river instead of out to sea? When did they drift up a creek on a high spring tide on a warm summer's evening? When did they sail between an island and a headland and look down through clear water to rocks just a couple of feet below? When, after a long day in the office, did they say, "We've got an hour before the wind dies, let's take the yacht for a sail."

They will think again and say that in a small boat I can't go as far as they can. But even that isn't true. You can load a small boat onto a trailer, hitch it to the car, and go down the road five, ten, or a hundred miles to new cruising grounds whenever the mood takes you.

But you can't go away overnight, they'll argue. And I will ask, why not? If you have the right boat, you can sail into a beach, pull up the boat, and make it fast to a tree, or with an anchor. Then you can offload the camping stove and the tent and settle down for the night. If the beach isn't suitable and you're not bothered about going ashore, you can drop the anchor, take out the thwarts, lay mattresses alongside the centerboard case, and pass the night being lulled by the water lapping against the hull.

Of course, for all these things, you do need the "right" boat. It has to be light enough to be towed behind a car and pulled up a beach without a trailer, but not so light that a night at anchor is miserable because you're bouncing around like a cork. It has to have a sailing performance spirited enough to be fun, but not so spirited that it's exhausting for anyone who hasn't followed Jane Fonda's latest workout torture. It must be capable of sailing in the smallest of breezes, but equally capable of taking a stiff blow in its stride. It must row reasonably well, be simple to rig, be comfortable to sail, have good storage spaces, and, above all, be a sheer pleasure to behold. Given all these things, you'd have the perfect boat.

It's the boat I've been subconsciously looking for all my life. And now, on paper at any rate, I've found her. She may not be the biggest boat in these pages, but she's the boat that I've been saving a name for: *Small*.

Small

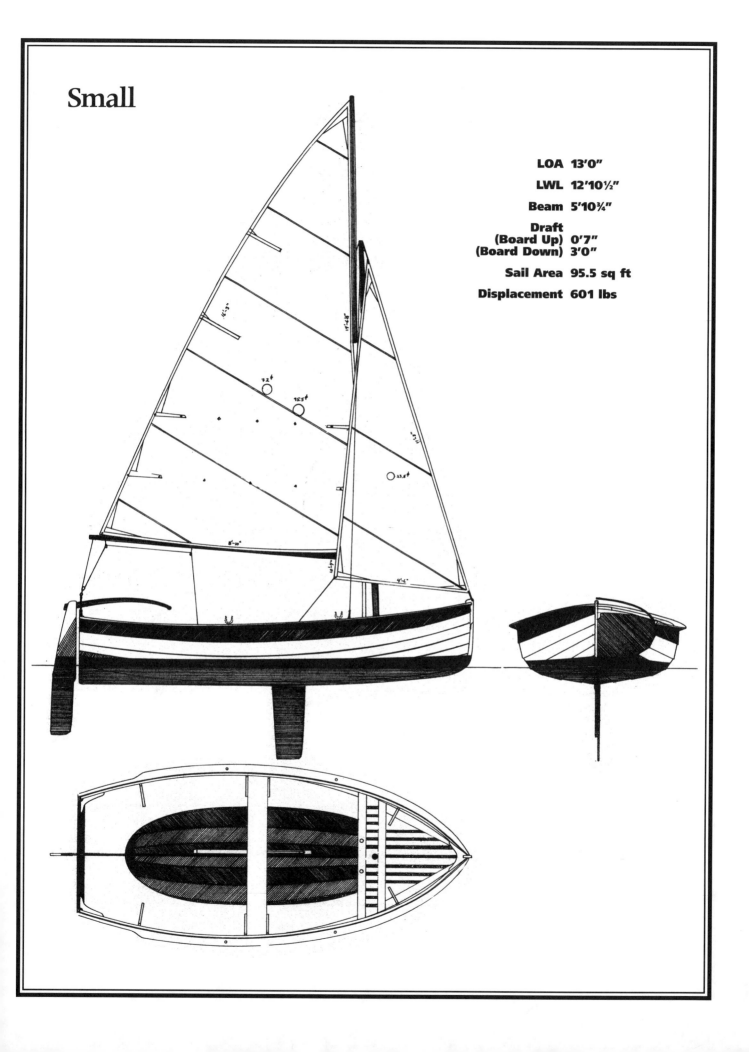

LOA 13'0"

LWL 12'10½"

Beam 5'10¾"

Draft
(Board Up) 0'7"
(Board Down) 3'0"

Sail Area 95.5 sq ft

Displacement 601 lbs

Small

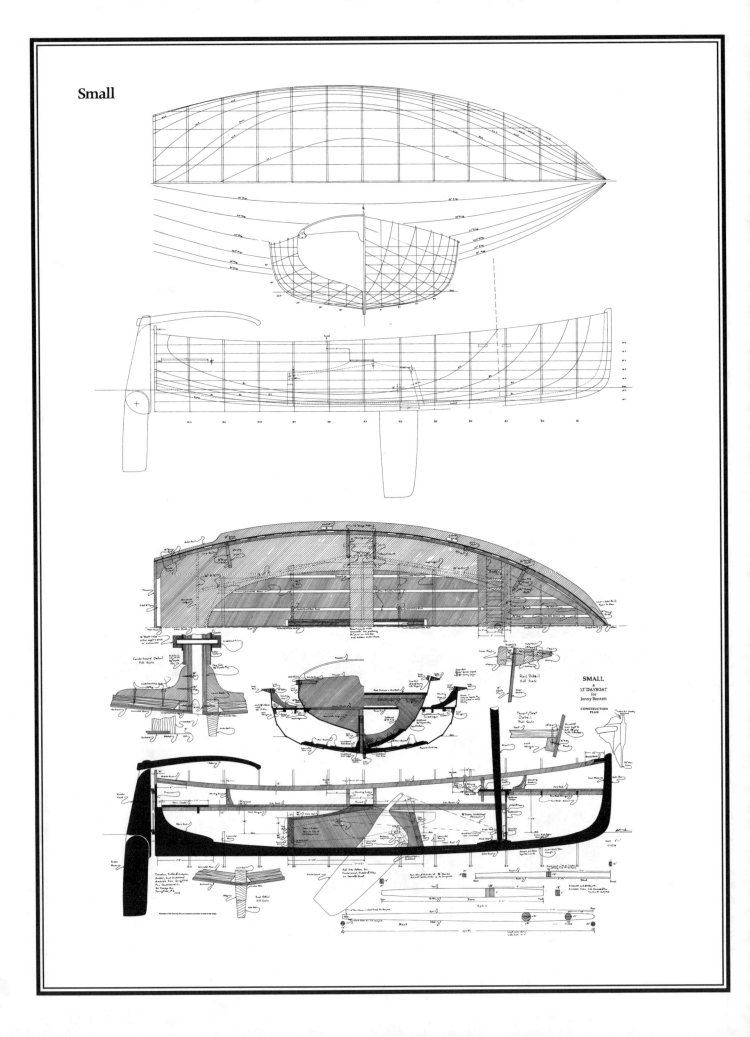

CHAPTER 2

23′ Indian Header

I met Peter Chesworth in March 1995 at the Maine Boatbuilders' Show in Portland, Maine, the same place where I met Jenny Bennett (see preceding chapter). He was representing *The Boatman* magazine. Since I had previously dealt with Pete Greenfield, editor of *The Boatman*, while writing an article about some designs inspired by Erskine Childers's book *Riddle of the Sands*, we already had a connection.

Peter, an Englishman, helped make history in recent British boating magazine publishing. With Pete Greenfield and Jenny Bennett, he was involved in the establishment of *Classic Boat*, a publication dedicated to traditional boats in Britain and beyond, regardless of age or building material. *Classic Boat* carried historical pieces written by the likes of John Leather, reviews of marine art and boat design, reports of sailing trials of new boats with traditional appeal, and exceptional editorials. When the magazine was taken over in Britain's publishing wars, the trio went on to start *The Boatman*, which also was eventually bought out. (Showing great singlemindedness and resilience, Pete Greenfield, Peter Chesworth's associate, went on to found a third title, *Water Craft*. Reminds me a bit of the Baron in "Monty Python and the

Holy Grail." He built a castle, it sank into the mud, then he built another castle, it too sank into the mud, but then he built a third castle....)

At our first meeting Chesworth talked of his dream of building a pocket cruiser to be owned jointly by a few couples. I showed him plans for Trooper, a 20-foot pilot sloop design, and discussed them with him. It was close to the kind of boat he was looking for—maybe a bit small for his needs, but a good starting point.

On his return to England, Peter wrote with more particulars. His friend Dick Phillips, now the head instructor at the Lyme Regis International School of Boatbuilding in Dorset, was then teaching at the Falmouth Industrial College in Cornwall. Dick was responsible for building boats featured in *The Boatman*, and the two were the core co-conspirators in the pocket-cruiser scheme. Referring to our discussions, Peter wrote:

Trooper

> Your description and reasoning for the design so matches Dick's and my thinking that it's unreal, I might need a little convincing as regards the solid-fuel stove as the only cooker, but I am sure we could meet somewhere near the idea. Everything else about the construction, handling, and concept of "modern" tabloid cruisers today, I have to say, is music to my ears. I absolutely agree that although your design is American, it certainly does not force the issue, indeed it appears to me to have the best of both worlds....It's refreshing to know someone like yourself who can pool different cultures and ideas together.

I wrote back to "set the hook" and discuss some of the points he had raised:

> I'm glad you enjoyed the pilot sloop drawings. Don't hesitate to share your thoughts with me even before you feel ready to commit to any formal agreement. It's useful to get qualified feedback on my boats. Outside influence helps fertilize the imagination. For your sake, it could pay off in getting the benefit of a longer percolation time.
>
> On the solid-fuel stove, it can take a Sterno insert for very informal warm-weather pot warming, or a single-or double-burner gas or alcohol stove can be mounted above it, or in its place, for the hot season. But I thought British sailing was always a wool-sweater-and-watch-cap affair?

Along with the pocket cruiser, Peter was intrigued with the idea of a beach cruiser. He had gone for a holiday in Scotland some years back during which he and his wife, Terie, had...

...borrowed an 18-foot Whammel boat from a good friend and boatbuilder, Bill Bailiff of Character Boats, to trail and sail around the coast off the Island of Mull, in the Inner Hebrides off the west coast of Scotland.... I had always...dreamed of one day sailing the lochs and sounds, enjoying the often breathtaking scenery and the sheer lonely beauty of the place.

It is, however, more than 800 miles by road from Cornwall, and a good two-to four-day passage by sea, and with time limited by work, especially in the summer, the idea of sailing up there is out of the question, even if I had a boat that could make the passage.

So, the six days with the Whammel were a very useful experiment in what was possible and what worked. The Whammel is completely open and has no centerboard, just a keel that runs the length of the boat, with a deep skeg aft. She is lug-rigged with a jib set on a short, removable, unstayed bowsprit. Her working-boat origins are very evident; she was stable and sailed well, was easy to rig, and rowed well.... Despite a pair of unmatched oars and her weight of around three-quarters of a ton, we rowed her back through a sea, golden in the color of the setting sun and as smooth as a sheet of glass.

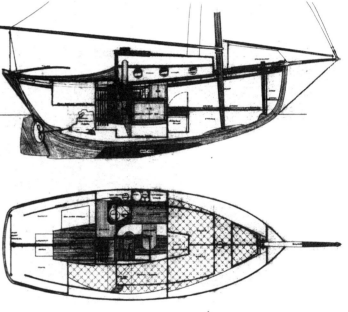

The experiment proved a resounding success. We had a fabulous time. We drove about the island and launched whenever the mood or the weather allowed, we sailed for a couple of hours (or nearly 15 one day), and we threw a tent and a stove in the boat and disappeared for three days to a little remote bay, where we didn't see another soul and it felt something like heaven on earth.

So, to the criteria for this instrument of escapism. Key words: simple, traditional, stable, and because of those things, it will be aesthetically pleasing. They always seem to go together somehow.

I would guess the ideal length to be about 17 or 18 feet. I really enjoyed not having a centerboard to clutter up the boat. I would like to be able to sleep aboard, so it would be good if the thwarts were removable, giving lots of room for mattress rolls and sleeping bags on the sole under a cockpit tent. I know convention will say you should have a small foredeck and a cuddy below to store bedding, etc., but we found on the Whammel—which had a locker in a tank in the bows—that being able to go virtually to the bows was a great advantage when coming into a beach. You are still in the boat, not balancing on the bows as you come through shore waves....

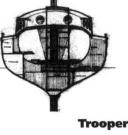

Trooper

The rig...on the Whammel...was standing lug with a jib. The mast was unstayed, solid and fitted into a cutout in the mast thwart, retained in place by a wooden wedge. The joy of such a system is speed and simplicity of rigging the craft. To illustrate the working origins of the beast, there wasn't a shackle on the boat.

Peter then went into greater detail on the boat we had discussed previously. The key to this boat was a "syndicate" ownership plan. Leaving aside the echoes of Woodstock, would it be possible for a set of close friends to own a boat together and use it cooperatively? If it is, there would be important advantages to the arrangement. Peter continued:

> If you remember, when we first met in Portland last March I was carrying a torch for the idea of a small, tabloid-type cruiser that would be owned by four couples but only sailed by one couple at a time. So, to all intents and purposes the boat would be theirs when they were on it.... [I've had] several conversations with many owners who...were moving down in size. The arguments that they used to justify going smaller work just as well for me trying to squeeze some sailing into a busy summer schedule. I also long to sail in many of the places I am lucky enough to visit in Europe, and I know that they will remain a dream unfulfilled if I don't plan carefully and own or part-own the right boat.

Peter then described a hypothetical cruise in this hypothetical boat from the south coast of England to Brittany:

> It's a 24-hour channel crossing from Falmouth. But there's the rub. If, and I emphasize if, the weather cooperates and is fair for a crossing on the first day of the holiday, you make the passage and sail down the coast for a few days, then the return passage starts to play on the mind. Can we go on that little bit more—if the wind were to stay in this direction...? So, after three or four days of carefree cruising down the coast, you are on your way back, starting to take more and more interest in the weather forecasts, and in the end you return to this side of the channel five days early, to beat the depressions that are coming across the Atlantic.
>
> Worse, of course, is getting it all wrong and doing some marathon nightmare crossing, which is usually followed by the now-familiar scene of loved ones kissing the earth (papal-like) after you row ashore with the soaking contents of the boat....

Peter returned again and again to the need to consider the desires of the sailor's spouse. With many couples, it's the husband who wants a boat, and the wife is uncertain. I agree with Lin Pardey and Annie Hill, two experienced sailors, on the subject: Too many sailing couples never get their "sea legs" because the woman's point of view isn't taken seriously.

Peter went on to describe the way the same two-week holiday would work out with the syndicated boat:

> Let's suppose we are the couple with the first two weeks. Drive, towing the boat, to the ferry; sleep a peaceful night while crossing the channel; awaken to a shower and a breakfast cooked by someone else; feel refreshed and full of anticipation of a fortnight's sailing in France.

The boat is craned into the water and rigged at a leisurely Breton pace, an operation probably broken with a decent lunch in the local auberge. A few little formalities remain. Return the car to the ferry terminal and catch a taxi back to the boat, stopping to purchase vast quantities of cheap wine, cheese, etc. Slip the crane driver a few francs for his trouble and sail gently down the coast a couple of miles on the last of the tide to a pleasant anchorage. Open the wine....

[Now you're free] to sail down the coast for two weeks as far or as little as desired. Remember only, on the penultimate day, to phone the next couple, to let them know where to meet you. Voila!—the next day your friends arrive, you take lunch together and tell of creeks and harbors, restaurants and cafes worth a visit. You drive the car back to the ferry port, board the ferry, have dinner, go to bed, wake up, and drive the car back home. Return to work happy, refreshed, and full of your exploits.

The couple you handed over to are by this time in somewhat of a dilemma. They are so impressed by your reports of the coast you have just cruised that they are now struggling, over a beautifully cooked dinner, with the decision of whether to sail farther south, as they had originally planned, or maybe retrace your cruise. The joy is it just does not matter which they choose.

It's all too good to be true, I hear you say, well I think it gets even better. Let's imagine for a moment that the weather turns ugly. Solution: Using public transport, return to the ferry port, collect the car, and tour—either using the boat for sleeping or staying in hotels.

If everyone goes south away from the ferry port, the only inconveniences are longer drives to meet the boat each time, and the last couple will have to nip back to the boatyard and pick up the trailer, haul out the boat, and drive back to the ferry. No real hardship, though, as the road distances are probably not that great.

Brittany, however, is no great adventure. My dream is to take the boat to such areas as the west coast of Norway, the Baltic, northern Spain, and the west coast of Scotland and the islands—none of which is possible with the very limited amount of time I would have in the normal scheme of things. But with the group boat, the possibilities go on and on.

Another plus, of course, is financial. All the running costs, transportation, charts, pilots, maintenance, and worries are cut into four, and that does make it more possible to enjoy.

I imagine the boat required to fulfill these dreams to be about 20 feet. It must look traditional and aesthetically appealing, and to this end I imagine a gaff cutter. The sailing characteristics should be friendly, by which I mean adequate performance, but it should sail upright; our ladies prefer it that way. The draft is not a great consideration; the idea of beaching and creek crawling is great, but actually doing it seems to create a lot of problems, both in design and execution. I would rather forgo a centerboard, which cuts the cabin in half, in favor of the space.

It must be trailerable but not necessarily a trailer-sailer; the weight would have to be somewhere between 1,000 and 1,500 kilograms [2,200 to 3,300 pounds], I suppose, to be able to tow it without the need for a truck. I would think that from the point of view of our building and the life the boat might lead, that strip-plank sheathed in mat, paint finished would be best. An engine is a must; we don't want to miss dinner because of a wind shift.

Accommodation—key word is comfortable. For a couple, in harbor or sheltered anchorage, a double berth would be cozy, as it is not anticipated that the berth(s) would be used at sea. Good-size, comfortable cockpit, lots of lounging in the sun. Cooking arrangements would only need to be simple—say, a two-ring and grill. Water tanks and sink, hell—we are on holiday. We want to eat ashore, or if we want to stay in some lonely anchorage, then the simple necessities are just fine. The heads. Now this is not only essential but probably the most difficult problem to resolve on a small cruising boat. Especially when the boat is owned by four couples. Whereas one couple might have no problem with the bucket-in-the-box solution, another may never set foot in the boat again unless they feel at ease with the facility on offer.

Above all, I think the boat must be comfortable for a couple who live together to be able to sail, sleep, and eat simply—without creating a home afloat crammed with all the trappings of an oceangoing cruiser. It's daysailing with civilized harbor accommodation.

I really like the way Peter has worked out this dream tour. It takes a lot of determination to build and own a boat, and it certainly helps to keep the "prize" firmly in mind through all the tribulations that life and the difficulties of the project throw at you.

Marsh Hawk

Understanding the way you, the owner, envision using a boat is very helpful to the designer, too. Your story produces a lot of information without the need to analyze and break it all down into a list of parameters. The designer then has a "picture" to work with. And, throughout the design process, you can return to your narrative for answers to the designer's questions. You may need to alter the narrative—in detail, or even broadly—but with this foundation to work from, no one will be making decisions arbitrarily.

Both Peter's options were intriguing. The beach boat concept is similar to my Marsh Hawk design, once featured in *Water Craft* magazine as a "how-to" series. The main difference is the centerboard. In the end, we decided to go with the "time-share" design. It became clear that the beach boat would interest Peter for a season, but the pocket cruiser was really under his skin. It's what I have heard called the "Pre R.I.P. boat"—as in "before I die." By the time many people have life worked out well enough to get to their dream boat, they are also old enough to have brought a lot of detail to the dream. Certain features become ingrained. They recognize that finding a way to bring it to reality is a life's goal, not just a passing whim.

The development of the design for Peter's boat fell into an elongated pace. I worked my way around my circle of commissions, including ones for paying clients, which left plenty of time for ideas to develop, strike passion, cool off, and invite reconsideration. Two years may seem like a long time to develop a design, and certainly it can be done in less, but I have always recommended that people start the process long before they think they're ready to begin construction.

There is a valuable period between the vague daydream and the imperative to be afloat next season. Too many people waste that time, thinking that until they are ready to start, there's no use getting serious. It's my contention that this is the time to work on the design. Earlier, there isn't much incentive, much pressure. After the hunger strikes, the mad rush has taken over, leaving no time for thoughtful consideration.

A long incubation period also spreads out the design fee, and allows time to establish a realistic budget. Financial planning can be worked out. Using time wisely can make all the difference between frustration and having your dreams realized.

Galena

I offered Peter two earlier designs as examples to consider. The first, *Galena*, was an early version of a design for an electric auxiliary, *Annabelle Two*, reviewed by Joel White in *WoodenBoat* magazine. *Galena* was reviewed in Mike O'Brien's *Boat Design Quarterly*. Then I wrote a letter to Peter synthesizing our various discussions:

> The design for your boat seems pretty well jelled in my mind and will just require fleshing out. I see the boat with a dark green hull, white boottop, and red bottom. The deck is buff, and the cabin sides, toerail, and coaming are oiled cherry, as is the curved raked transom. The varnished spars are white at their ends. The whole effect is traditional American, with the cutter rig worked in.
>
> We're looking for a boat that comes out of the tradition of the working vessels of New England. If we went no farther than the obvious, I'd be drawing you a Friendship sloop. But I'm afraid the Friendships lack interior space, and the aesthetic possibilities are limited to what is now nearly a cliche. It's not that I don't like the type. The problem is that the Cape Cod catboat and the Friendship sloop

are the only traditional types we ever see. We've loved them to death and relegated other types to museums.

Some lesser-known types—such as the Kingston lobsterboat of Massachusetts Bay, along with the Friendship sloop—were the poor man's Banks schooners. Then, as now, emulation of the "big boys" was common. I find it much more interesting to go to the original sources of inspiration and make my own reinterpretations. I've pored over Howard Chapelle's *The American Fishing Schooners* for more than 20 years. As a study of evolution, it's unsurpassed in naval architecture, chronicling the rise and development of a passing lineage. Now it's almost gone, along with New England's Banks fisheries.

Annabelle

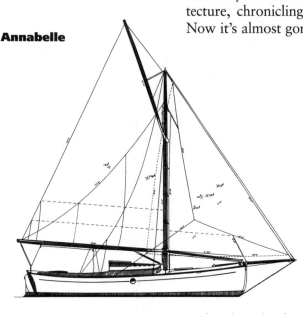

My earliest memories are enlivened by the sights and smell of that fishery. When I was little, five or six, my father would take me with him to Town Wharf in Provincetown, Massachusetts, where he visited with his fisherman friends. They never let us leave without filling our trunk with cod as big as I was.

At least once a summer, we went out on an ex-rumrunner, *Cee-Jay*, for a day of deep-sea fishing. I remember my father's wool-trousered leg beside me as I held his hand on the gangway, and the rail and scupper of the boat as we walked aft. Low tide had the boat in deep shadow next to the tall, tarred pilings. It was dark and mysterious under the wharf. The water, a deep emerald green alternating with indigo, was lit from below by pulsating shafts of gold. The surface was iridescent with fish oils and diesel waste. Dancing in the water, caught by refraction, slivers of silver and green sea smelts darted past; starfish as big as a hand climbed on the piles; and the pale, glowing orbs of sea clam shells, like dinner plates, loomed off the bottom.

The underside of the wharf created an echo chamber. The hard surfaces of water and wood reverberated with idling engines, and the shimmering fall of ice-melt dripped off the edge of the wharf high above. Shouts and the slamming of fish crates on concrete rang out from the warehouse above.

The smells of the wharf: fresh fish, gurry, diesel fumes, and the haunting aroma of tarred cod-lines hanging along the edges of the hurricane deck. Quahogs and dead white squid were piled on the bait table, waiting to be cut into chunks to sweeten the 3-inch hooks ballasted with sash weights on the end of wire leaders.

I held on as the hawsers were cast off. The easy roll of the deck was replaced by the push and pull of inertia as the boat backed and filled, leaving her berth. The engines cycled from neutral to forward, to reverse and back; gouts of wash foamed up alongside the hull or shot backward at sharp angles, the foam hissing sharply.

Strong, bright sunlight cut the shadows, then suddenly erupted into a clear horizon as we left the pier behind. The sun was warm, but the cool of the water, now a rush of blue and green foam tinged with violets and maroons, radiated more powerfully—as cold as the steel cans of Ballantine's my father and his friends were cracking with a rusty opener. I still see the view through a scupper, as light and shadow rose and fell with the swell. The roar of the engines, wide open, without beginning or end....

If I had grown up in Maine, I might be fulfilled drawing Friendship sloops. As it is, I find excuses to downplay their significance and prefer to follow the trail back to the schooners.

The other drawing is based on the Indian Header, a type developed by Thomas McManus of Boston. Indian Header refers to a series of schooners McManus built for a single owner; all were named after New England Indian chiefs. They shared certain hull characteristics, most notably the curve of the stem. While not that popular with fishermen, who preferred more burdensome hulls, harbor pilots valued them more for their ease of handling and speed, rather than carrying capacity.

A smaller class of similar boats for the inshore fisheries, no slouches at 60 to 70 feet, were called "sloop boats." They were rigged as double-headsail gaff sloops. Instead of combining an American hull with a British rig, I've used this sloop-boat rig on your boat. I haven't drawn an interior yet; Trooper's will fit. I'm waiting for your "corrected" print before going back into the interior.

As I've mentioned, some of the schooners bore the names of Indian chiefs from Massachusetts tribes. Or they were named after members of the owner's family—either singly or in pairs—or after the owners themselves. My favorite in the Provincetown fleet, a boat still fishing today, is the early transitional dragger with a fine counter stern and an Indian Header's bow: *Gilbert & Roland*. I know I'm entering potentially dangerous ground here suggesting names, but perhaps yours might be named after Squanto. He was an American Indian who had traveled to England, learned the language, returned to what would eventually become Massachusetts, and greeted the Pilgrims when they landed at Cape Cod in their native tongue.

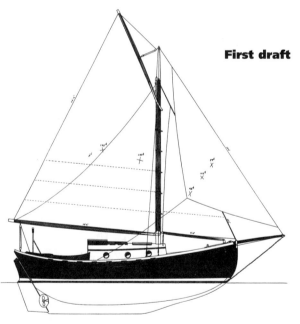

First draft

A designer doesn't just make visible what's expected; he (or she) needs to explore variants of what's been considered. It's easy to speculate about changes, but unless we see how they look, in some detail, we can't judge their suitability.

Fine-tuning the size of a boat is a tricky proposition. People don't shrink, just because we want a boat to be smaller. As size decreases, seaworthiness is lost by virtue of scale—waves are proportionately larger and hull speed slower. If you have a size limit in mind, it needs to be analyzed to see what is at stake to achieve it.

I like to draw a "relaxed," longer variant of most boats, and I did this with Peter's, stretching the hull to 24 feet. This is easily done with the Maxsurf design program by changing the overall dimensions in a dialog box. (See illustrations on pages 38 & 39.) Since the boat is to be longer, but not greater in displacement, adjustments are made to take advantage of the greater length. As a boat gets longer, it need not be as beamy, or as full in the sections.

I sent the new drawings to Peter with these comments:

Counter-sterned variant

This one is 24 feet on deck. The displacement is similar, maybe a bit lighter than the 23-footer. It dawned on me that the kind of trailering you plan to do doesn't end at a ramp. I know you've been telling me that all along. The draft isn't controlled by the distance you're able to back into the water. Weight, not length, is the major controlling factor. If you're willing to haul 5,500 pounds, 4 percent longer shouldn't matter much on the road.

And the result is a better boat afloat, where it matters. The short counter draws out the run. I've lowered the freeboard and lessened the curvature of the sheer a bit. The lower house retains the 4-feet plus sitting headroom. The rig is unchanged except for less steeve to the bowsprit, and the traveler ring for the jib, as requested.

In May 1996, my wife, Kay, and I visited Peter and his accomplice Dick Phillips in Cornwall, a very nautical corner of the world. After the port, Stilton, and walnuts, I brought out the drawings. Short of a launching party, this is my favorite part of creating a design, showing a client the latest results: excitement over the way the boat is shaping up, the client's enthusiasm, and the debate over changes lasting late into the evening. On our return to the States, I wrote a letter to Peter with a synopsis of the points he, Dick, and I covered:

Twenty-four feet is just too long. It crosses that physical and psychological line between a large, trailerable boat and a trailering liability. You seem to favor returning to a modified version of the 23-footer with a bit less sheer and the rig of the 24-footer. Dick and I lean toward a re-proportioned 23-foot version of the 24-foot hull.

I want to sketch out both alternatives and start working on the interior, checking to see if three berths with a private head can work in either version. The transom-stern boat is more likely to have the most useful interior space, but I think the counter stern can be made to work. It could be worth the slightly more complicated construction to produce a hull with more balanced ends and more exciting looks.

I want to see whether the displacement, and thus the trailer weight, in both hulls can't be brought down a bit. It's easy to point at length as an impediment on the road, but weight can be a bigger problem. The 3-foot 6-inch draft is a good figure. Since the boat is intended to be launched by crane, depth on a slipway is not a controlling factor.

While I remain a fan of British and European boats, it was enlightening to see that the most beautiful boats when we visited the Festival of the Sea in Bristol were *Pride of Baltimore II* and an Alden schooner. I think you said so yourself? It bolsters my conviction that your boat should be "quintessentially American" in appearance.

When the new drawings were ready, I wrote to Peter again:

In my last letter, I mentioned an ambitious program of feasibility studies and alternative plans. Enclosed is one version only. It's in my nature to spin out variables into infinity, but if this design spiral isn't to end up looking like the Andromeda Galaxy, there must be a limit. Both for the sake of expediency and to exercise my own judgment, I've decided the counter-stern version was too extreme. It wasted waterline length, complicated construction, and lost volume over the transom stern. Besides, the transom stern was your preference.

Displacement has been whittled down to 5,300 pounds. The prismatic coefficient is .54, which I consider an optimum number. The displacement/length ratio is 282, at the high end of the medium range—again, a good place to be in a small cruiser, where capacity needs to be high. The sail area/displacement ratio is 17.4, at the upper edge of moderate. Sail area is the "horsepower" of the boat. Too many traditional cruisers have a reputation for sluggishness simply because they are undercanvased. The ballast/displacement ratio, with 2,300 pounds of ballast, is 43 percent, a generous amount considering it's set for the actual displacement, not an ideal racing one; the water tanks are low and will add to the righting moment. The Dellenbaugh angle, a measure of stiffness rating the hull and rig together, is 16.8—quite stiff. We could probably safely increase the sail area. I'm using American norms for this, expecting lower average wind speeds than you'll be dealing with....Let's stay with the area shown.

These figures indicate a boat relatively fast in moderate-to-stronger winds, provided seas don't peak up. It's only a 23-foot boat! The stiffness may be a bit much, but it will be easy to spoil by raising the center of gravity if the roll is too snappy. A small boat needs stiffness. It's such a big world out there! A drifter or an asymmetrical spinnaker is the best way to boost sail area for light airs, and the engine needs to earn its keep.

The enclosed head you've requested is shown. You need to assess realistically the merits of a very small enclosed compartment versus the loss of space. This interior should work, but the head compartment is cramped. I've seen worse on small stock cruisers, and it's an advantage to be able to "wedge" yourself in the head in a seaway, but....

The alternative is to raise the seat in the vee of the forward berths and put the head there. For privacy, others are relegated to the cock-

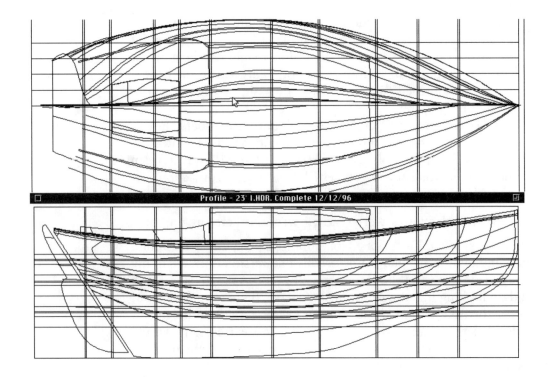

Profile - 23' I.HDR. Complete 12/12/96

Screen shots of the 23' Indian Header from Maxsurf and Hydromax

The upper views are from Maxsurf and show how the traditional drawing views appear on screen. The lower drawings are from Hydromax, the part of Maxsurf that computes hydrostatics. The heeled perspective view (right) incorporates information from a "Load Case" spreadsheet and shows the hull at "Hull Speed."

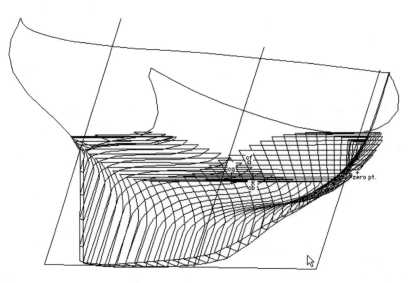

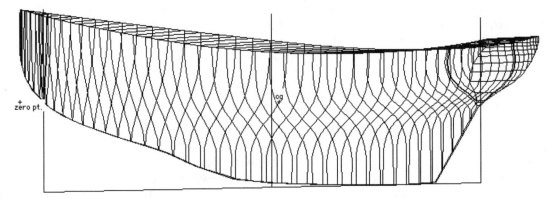

38

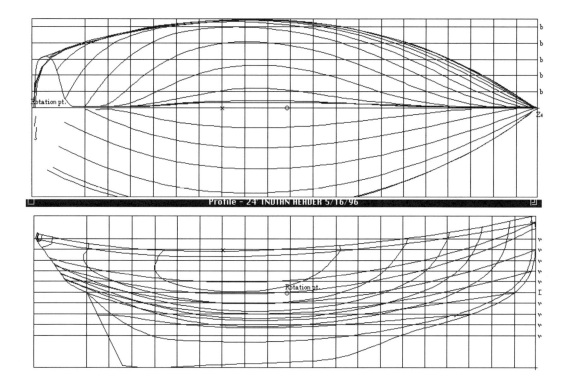

Profile - 24' INDIAN HEADER 5/16/96

Screen shots of the 24' Indian Header from Maxsurf and Hydromax

The 24-footer was started by just typing in the new length, and then the new hull was worked to create the counter stern. At right is a view created in Hydromax, which can be compared to the similar view of the 23 footer. The view at the bottom is a shaded perspective created in Maxsurf. This allows one to get a clear picture of the "model" and can be rotated on all three axes.

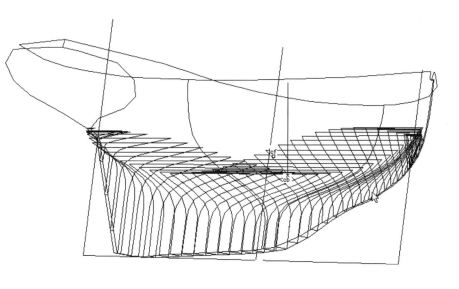

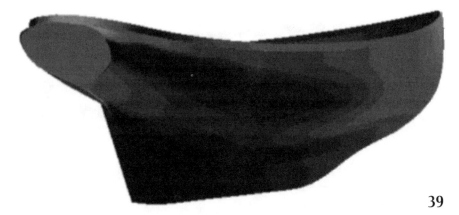

pit until further notice. The whole interior is then the "head compartment." It's spacious and airy without sacrificing any accommodation space. I'll do what I'm told on this count.

Otherwise, I think the interior works out well. There's ample sitting headroom. The counter has a two-burner propane stove and it's covered by a cutting board for charts. With a removable table amidships, three can sit and eat. A basin is built into the countertop in the head, and there's a wet locker behind the toilet under the bridge deck, next to the engine.

The cockpit seats are long and wide enough to stretch out on for lounging or for sleeping in good weather. The space underneath is fitted with lockers for sails and fenders, etc. A propane locker vents through the transom.

I think we're getting somewhere with this version. It's shorter, more in keeping with the practical and psychological limits of a trail-

Closing in on final draft: smaller club-footed staysail than in final version

40

erable vessel. The required accommodations fit. The rig is powerful, yet snug and easily reduced. And the boat looks "American."

Shortly after writing the above letter, I met with Peter at Mystic, Connecticut, and then he spent nearly a week with us in our home. Naturally, we found time to "talk boats" and to go over the Indian Header in detail. After Peter left, I wrote to him to summarize the situation:

> The most salient point in our discussions was choosing the two-berth interior. Since the boat is to be sailed by a couple exclusively, the added space is best utilized by increasing the galley. We'll transpose the head to starboard and place the galley aft on the port side. This makes cooking in the companionway easiest for right-handed people.
>
> We are considering the possibility of having to shorten the boat to 21 feet 6 inches for ease of trailering and as an economizing measure. The two-berth interior adapts well to the shorter length. If we do this, we will in fact be returning close to the original prototype, Trooper, the 20-foot pilot sloop I first showed you more than a year ago.
>
> A 25-foot version of the design naturally follows, for people with no need to trailer long distances. This type of "evolutionary" development appeals to me, with each design begetting a line of related designs.
>
> In the rig, I'm happy to see the abandonment of the self-tending

Closing in on the accommodations

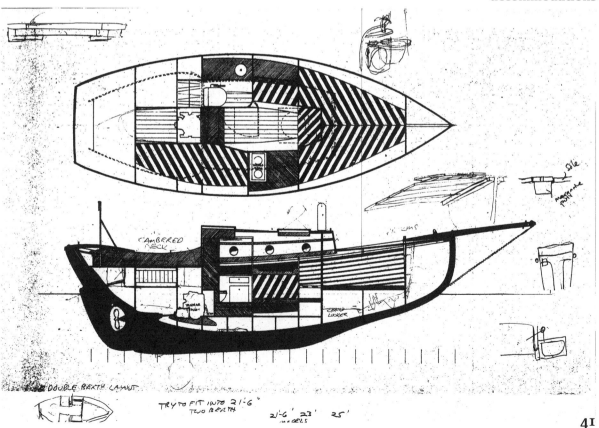

staysail in favor of one with a slight overlap. With a small boat, it's hard to justify a double-headsail rig from a sail efficiency standpoint. By maximizing the size of the staysail, we increase its efficiency and add area down low directly amidships. The increased slot effect helps the main....Foresail travelers tend to be a nuisance.

The main sets with lacing instead of hoops, making it easier to raise and lower the mast for transport. The halyards are brought to a pinrail ahead of the mast. The slight inconvenience of going forward is offset by the greater leverage possible in sweating them up. We have reconfirmed our commitment to a winch-free boat. The mainsheet is changed from a traveler to a double-ended sheet, allowing the tiller to be pivoted up and lashed to the gallows to clear the cockpit. The peak halyard sets to a bridle on the gaff.

The bobstay is set up with a tackle, British style, so the bowsprit can be reeved afloat. The gammon iron is hinged on one side. All the hardware is galvanized steel, with the exception of the tabernacle. It's sand-blasted stainless to limit rust caused by wear. The rigging is galvanized flexible 1x19 wire, and light boards for electric running lights are set up to the shrouds. The crosstrees are wood, in the traditional American pattern: a straight wooden spreader aft of the mast braced by a curved piece ahead, all secured to hounds on either side of the mast. Blocks are wooden and small scale.

The chain locker is in the after bay under the V-berth. The chain pipe is 4-inch plastic conduit. The skylight hatch has a round Lexan pane set in a galvanized or bronze finishing ring. The hatch cover is hinged on both ends so the hatch can be opened for ventilation in either direction. The opening portlights are bronze. The side ports are 6 inches in diameter. Two smaller, 4-inch or 5-inch lights are in the front of the house. They are laid out so they mitigate the "Thomas the Tank Engine" look.

A removable table is rigged between the settees and can be used in the cockpit. It stows under a removable section of the bunk flat. On the galley bulkhead is a small shelf with a water pump connected to the freshwater tank. The pump can be directed over the counter or to a hinged bracket holding a removable basin that drains into a bucket.

The bridge deck has an engine hatch cover that fits through the hatch for removal. Above the engine, a removable tray holds assorted gear easy to hand. The fuel tank is under the longer cockpit well. Water and waste tanks are under the cabin sole and under the settees. The cockpit deck is cambered like the main deck and is done in teak-veneered plywood, custom cut to look like laid teak. The main deck and housetop are in three layers of ¼-inch cedar. The lower layer is V-grooved running fore-and-aft, then two 45-degree diagonal layers. It's covered in Dynel set in epoxy for a "canvas" deck.

Decks and the hull planking are filleted and taped to the bulkheads. The deck-to-bulkhead seams are covered by molding strips hiding the fillets. The visible parts of the hull in the cabin are ceiled in cedar, which is screwed to false ribs laminated to the hull. This keeps the fastenings out of the hull laminates, eliminating risk of moisture penetration. The hull is planked in white cedar strips, either bead-and-cove or "Speed-Strip." The lighter weight of white cedar wins out over Douglas-fir, even though it is harder to obtain in Britain.

In the lazarette is a propane locker open to the transom. The forward bulkhead has openings to stow the ballooner and some empty plastic water jugs. Last but not least, there's a circular well in the cabin sole fitted with a removable cover the size of a plastic margarine cup—an easy-to-empty receptacle for sweepings.

We also came up with a color scheme in keeping with the type. The hull is a dark, bottle green; "National Trust Green" is the British rough equivalent. The bottom is "Copper-Bot." The boottop is in two parts—a lower red band and a wider, tapered white one. The cabin sides and interior surfaces are ivory white. The deck and cabintop are a sandy buff. The bulwark is white, and a yellow or gold cove stripe echoes the sheer.

The rubrail, coaming, cabintop molding, companionway, forehatch, and transom are varnished or oiled cherry. The spars are oiled and varnished Douglas-fir (Oregon pine, as it's called in Britian), with white tips. The sails are "Egyptian" dacron.

We had also discussed a tender for the boat. Back in 1976, Eric Dow, a Maine boatbuilder, and I had built a 22-foot Friendship sloop to my design—my first major commission. Then Eric built a little peapod for the owner to use as a tender. I think it was Pete Culler who said that a small cruiser that's unable to carry a tender on deck needs a seaworthy dinghy that can take care of itself in bad weather. This peapod was definitely that kind of tender.

Peter had shamefacedly admitted he was just planning on having an inflatable. One look, and one word—*peapod*—was enough to change his mind. I started the design that week and sent Peter a Maxsurf printout of the basic hull form shortly thereafter. Soon came his reaction:

> I couldn't reply before now as I was waiting to show Dick the beautiful peapod.... Bloody lovely, it's absolutely beautiful. Dickie and I sat in the pub on Thursday night and waxed lyrical about the beautiful shape and the jaunty sheer, and basically we had a grand evening staring at your lines. You clever chap, I wish I could create such beautifully elegant shapes. So Dick and I are over the moon with the little beauty; I am itching to have the time in the near future to build a scale model of her.

Little open boats can be the most difficult to design. Not only do they require almost as much work as a large boat, for a substantially reduced fee, but since they are simple and uncovered, every detail has so much impact on the overall aesthetic of the boat. This is particularly true of a wooden boat built with a nontraditional technique. On a cruising sailboat, a certain amount of its structure can be hidden from immediate view without altering one's sense of the boat, or the way it's put together. But that's not the case with a small open boat.

You expect to see ribs, and there's tremendous impact from the way the rails and floorboards are done. But there's only so much you can do to "simulate" carvel or clinker construction before the boat becomes hopelessly compromised, neither fish nor fowl. The solution lies in working out an alternative that has an appeal of its own. The construction needs to have a consistency and rationale while reflecting,

The peapod

or echoing, the expectations set up by the standards of traditional construction. These issues were a major part of the struggle I had with Jenny Bennett's *Small*, and they also affected Peter's peapod.

The question of reserve buoyancy brought it all to a head. A wooden boat will float swamped, but if additional buoyancy is provided, it can also float its crew. My search for answers took some twists and turns, which I reported to Peter:

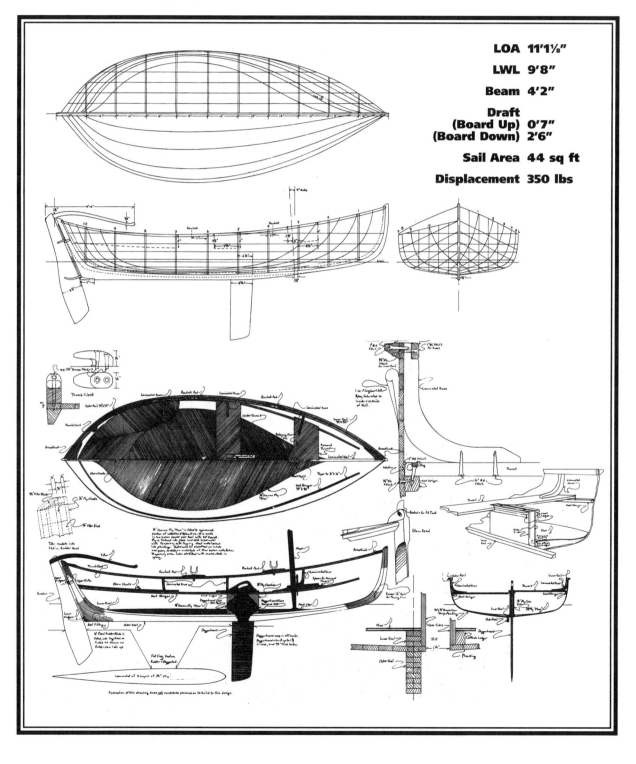

LOA	**11′1⅛″**
LWL	**9′8″**
Beam	**4′2″**
Draft (Board Up) (Board Down)	**0′7″** **2′6″**
Sail Area	**44 sq ft**
Displacement	**350 lbs**

I've finalized the rig, 32 square feet in the spritsail main and 12 square feet in the jib. The seating is made up of two thwarts—one forward, one amidships—and curved stern sheets.

The hull will provide 72 pounds of buoyancy; the daggerboard, about 30 pounds. The boat should weigh about 85 pounds, not counting the rig. This leaves about 17 pounds of surplus positive buoyancy. If the seats are made up of 2 inches of foam sandwiched between $\frac{1}{8}$ inch plywood, we gain another 125 pounds of buoyancy, for a total of 142 pounds of positive flotation. That's almost enough buoyancy to float the occupants in a swamped condition.

How do we gain another 50 pounds of flotation? We can side-step the issue by specifying flotation bags, or building tanks into the ends. Bags are very good on a trailered daysailer, but they can be a problem in a tender, where they're prone to theft and will be exposed to the weather for prolonged periods. Built-in tanks hide the boat's structure and have a "fiberglass look."

The seats are 2 inches thick, and even though the edges can be disguised by chamfers, they'll also have that fiberglass look. My other suggestion is also a bit questionable aesthetically. I propose a false bottom, a football-shaped $\frac{1}{8}$-inch plywood "floor" glued into the boat. It spans the inner keel and is about 3 feet 6 inches at the widest point. The hollow is filled with foam, and it's feathered into the hull, filleted, and taped. This is used in some glued-lap canoes and takes the place of floors, sawn or laminated, leaving a clean and simple interior and providing a lot of flotation.

The seats I'm proposing will give the boat a super-clean look without any interior structure, but they can detract from the aesthetics of the boat. An epoxy-and-fiberglass surface replaces the easily renewed "immortality" of traditional wood seats and floorboards. Wooden seats age gracefully and can always be "wooded" and restored to their original condition. This modern type of surface, while structurally in keeping with the hull, removes the overall feel of the boat a few steps farther from the classic ideal.

Structural questions are never far removed from aesthetic ones. In a pleasure boat, they are intrinsically wedded, since they are both important to the enjoyment of the boat. We can go with solid wood thwarts, and floorboards attached to laminated or sawn floors. Along with the rails, these can be varnished or oiled. Flotation can be provided by bags, or just ignored; the boat won't sink! This solution combines the look of a traditional wooden boat with the convenience of a strip or glued-lap hull.

The rails, spars, and tiller are still accents of wood. The seats and the floor must be very well done to look their best. It's counterintuitive, but wooden seats and floorboards take less finesse in finishing than a taped and 'glassed plywood structure. Any wavy edges of 'glass, or blips of resin, are quite unsightly and spoil the clean look.

Appearance is mediated by countless details. In a small boat, there are just a few details and all of the structure shows, leaving fewer opportunities to "dress up" the design. All the basics must look right, and be built right.

After a barrage of e-mail, I finally got an answer from Peter to my question about buoyancy:

> We favor tree-wood thwarts and stern sheets, with the clean foamed floor, whilst taking on board your comments regarding the need to get it absolutely perfect. I feel sure we can do a good job there, and I can even think of a few ways of disguising any defects (heaven forbid). As you suggest, we would varnish or oil the seats and the rail and tiller. As for any lack of buoyancy, tell them we will use bags (the ones under our eyes); that should satisfy the worriers. Scream if we are still missing something you need to know, and have pity on a mere virgin in these uncharted waters of design.

I got right down to it and finished up the drawings. After receiving the final drafts for the peapod and the Indian Header, Peter sent me his summation:

> It really is amazing how it's all come together. From a casual conversation...to the lines of the Indian Header.... I am a lucky chap....
>
> I have always been...able to see the form of a hull from lines, but my like or dislike is based purely on a gut feel. I suppose it harks back to the old adage, "If it looks right, etc."...I feel very privileged to have been connected with a designer who listened and understood my naive, often vague, wish list—and comprehended so well the concept of the boat and its use. To be able to guess my taste in aesthetics is tantamount to magic, as so much was unspoken.
>
> I think the peapod tender illustrates this very well. There we were chewing over the fine detail of the Indian Header on your drawing board and you asked me what I would do for a tender. My silence, and your realization that I was trying to think of a way of telling you that an inflatable would be practical.... Before I had time to spit out some lame reasoning, you had already decided that I should have a far more sensitive and beautiful companion.... So how did you know that my weakness was for peapods? Without further ado, you were back at [work] designing this "little belter."
>
> So to the main course. It's hard to put into words, something that so beautifully meets all my criteria. As we both know, boat design is always a compromise, but I think you grasped the essence of our idea for a "time-share" boat, knowing that we had prioritized the important features and were prepared to sacrifice others. I just knew it would be pleasing to the eye; a quick glance at some of your other designs assured me that she would look the part. Your understanding of "our" priorities was a great relief. I must admit when you first mooted the possibility of designing the boat, I had some concerns that my bluff might be called, and my "looks-good" philosophy might be put to the test.... I soon realized that I need not have worried, as we have now spent more time together, airing our thoughts and ideas not only on boat design but also on life in general. It became obvious we have a great deal in common.
>
> Overall, I adore the shape of the hull. From her sexy stern to her proud bow, the rig is going to be handy in every respect—stowable,

pretty, and easily handled. She generally looks like a happy boat, if you know what I mean. She has the look of a self-assured, content, mature, well-behaved, fun-loving character—just perfect for her intended use. And she should be as much at home in the Baltic as in Brittany, Scotland, or The Netherlands. The combination of European and American origins will stand her in good stead for the international waters for which she's intended. One thing is definite—no matter where she sails, she will always be admired by those with an eye for a good line.

...I do like the cockpit, perfect for those balmy evenings with glass in hand, looking out.... The shape and the angle of the coaming are great, combined with the superstructure to give a practical, good-looking, workable layout. The clear side decks give easy access forward.

Before I lurch off again, thinking of kicking the anchor over in some idyllic bay bathed in the late evening light of the midnight sun, let's get below. You were very constrained to do anything very dif-

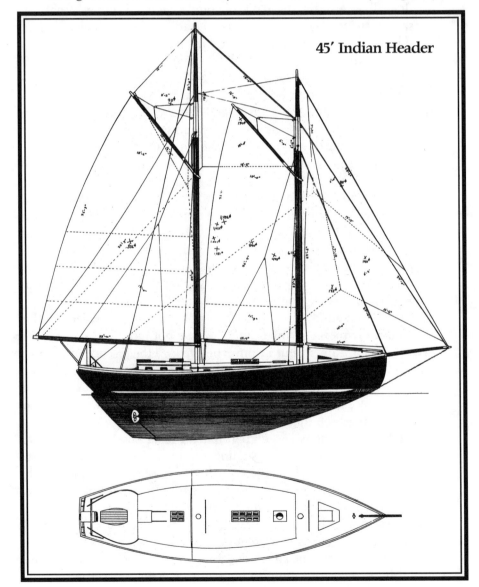

45' Indian Header

ferent here, but I do think the arrangement will be just dandy. Again, you really did take on board, literally, the entire raison d'etre, and I think a (mature) couple will enjoy the comfort and practicality of the design.

So, on the whole I think you have done a fantastic job, bringing a dream to the first stage of reality. All it remains for me to do now is to make the money to get building. The whole experience has been great. As I said, I had my doubts about having to articulate my wish list, but thanks to your ability to listen and prompt, and your skill as a designer, you have brought off a great project....

I suppose you would accept an invitation to cruise on our dream ship?

Notwithstanding Peter's enthusiastic response, a few questions remain. Can the syndicate/time-share idea really work? It's up to the individuals involved. Limiting it to two couples should give it a better chance than trying to coordinate the lives and interests of four couples. The costs are doubled with only two, but the interpersonal dynamics are greatly simplified.

The question of the head compartment will be left to the mock-up stage. Before any boat is fitted out inside, the interior should be laid out in mock-up. Some cardboard, plywood, and a glue gun will give you an idea of how the proposed interior will fit. Then it's possible to fine-tune heights and widths. If some aspect doesn't work, it can be caught and modified before expensive materials have been cut. The 3-D CAD work doesn't eliminate the need for the mock-up stage; nothing on a small, flickering screen can equal the benefit of actually "walking through" a mock-up interior. Not only is this stage a revelation for the designer, but it also is the best aid for the owner, who's often not so adept at abstract visualization.

As I've mentioned, this design can breed a family of related boats ranging from 20 feet to 40 feet and beyond. All will share the profile— a combination of short overhangs and a long waterline. The boats are easy to build and have a lot of capacity for a given length. Rigs can range from gaff sloop to schooner in the larger sizes. A Bermudian rig might work as well in some cases. While the design will never be as well known as the Friendship sloop, I'm convinced that Indian Headers can be wholesome additions to the traditional boat family.

23′ Indian Header

LOA 23′2″
LWL 20′5″
Beam 8′2″
Draft 3′6″
Sail Area 343 sq ft
Displacement 5,200 lb

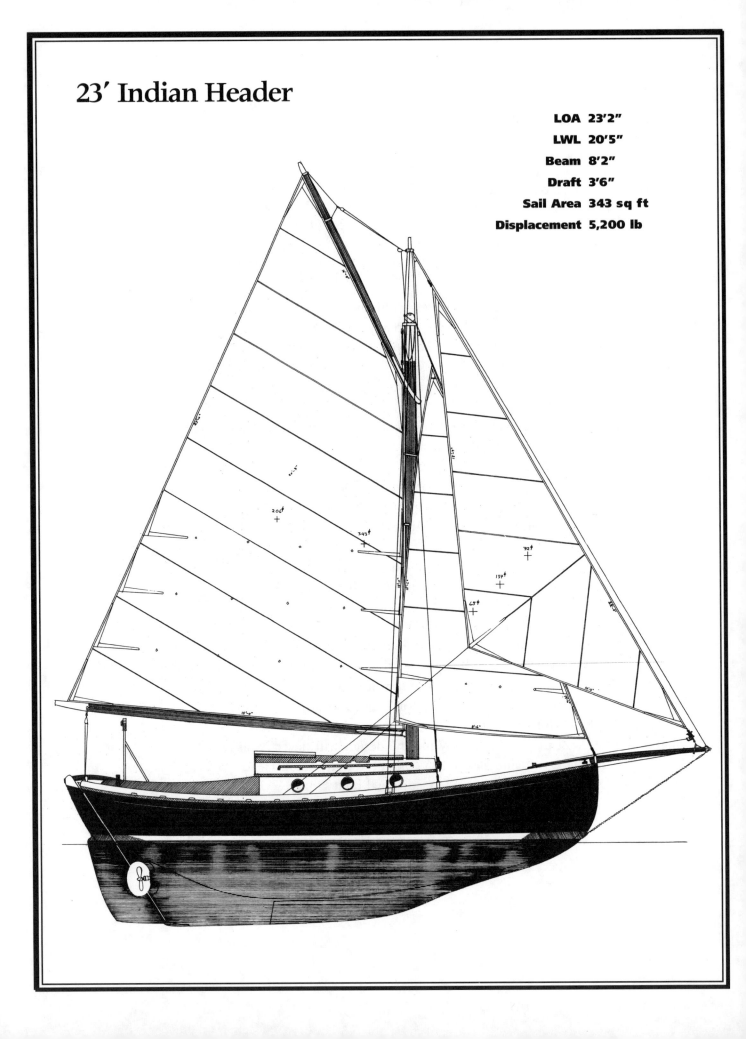

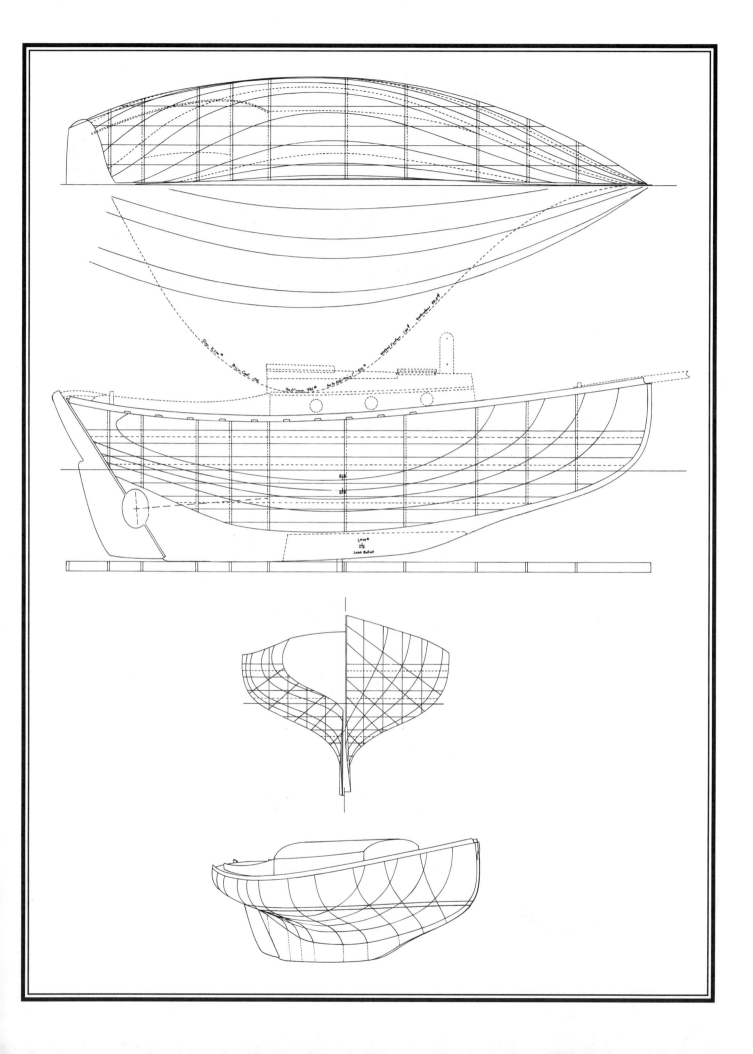

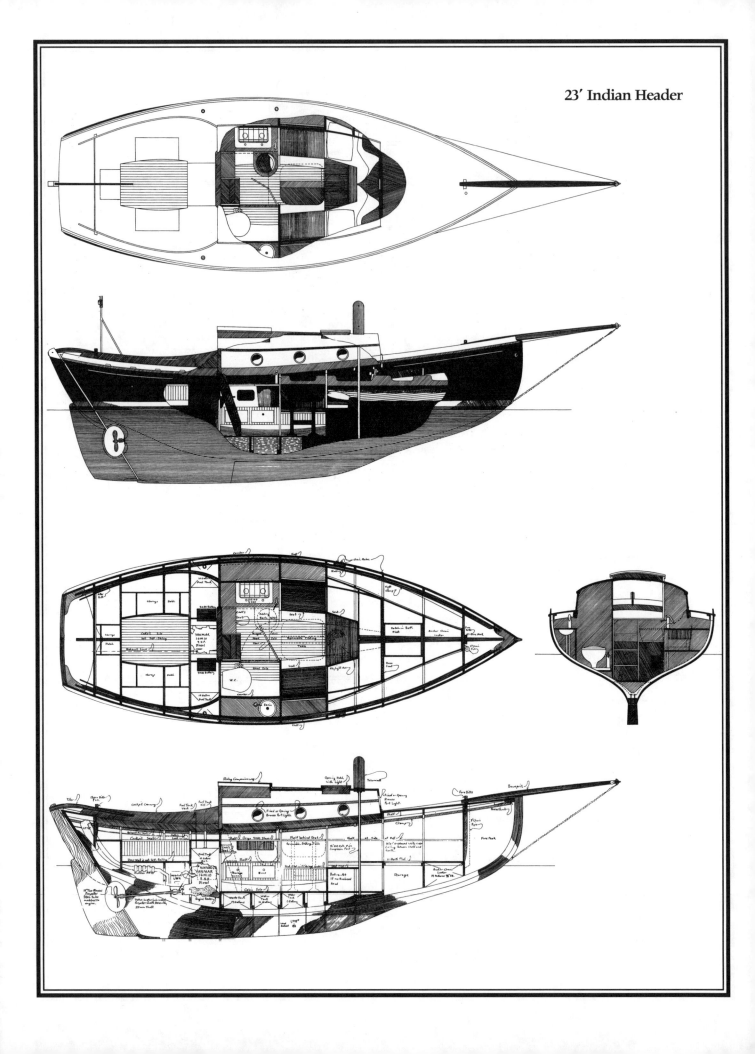

23' Indian Header

CHAPTER 3

40' Cruising Cutter

In August of 1995, I taught a course at WoodenBoat School in Brooklin, Maine, where John and Dee Deegan were in charge of the WoodenBoat waterfront. Infectiously good-humored, they worked together with the ease of a couple who've spent years sailing together. John is from Australia, Dee from the U.S., and they've voyaged extensively, including a 5½-year circumnavigation.

The Deegans had seen my design booklet, and the hulls of two of my boats were being built in classes at the school that week. My own boat, *Harry*, a 14-foot daysailer, was on one of WoodenBoat's moorings. When Kay and I returned to Brooklin later that summer, we sat on the grass by the waterfront and discussed the Deegans' future plans. After first returning to Australia, they were going on another voyage aboard their 43-foot Maurice Griffiths cutter *Sotalia*. They would spend a few years crossing the Pacific, going through the Panama Canal, and ending up in Brooklin again. After that, they hoped to build a new boat incorporating the fruits of their experiences. As the tide came in, we agreed that I would design it.

Dealing with the logistics of long-range communications, and keeping track of their wanderings, on top of the usual work involved

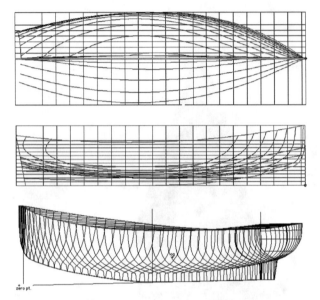

Screen shots of first draft from Maxsurf and Hydromax

in any new design, promised to be a challenge. A few months later, John sent specifications from Australia. The boat should be 40 feet long with a 12 foot beam and a shallow draft—3 feet 6 inches. The Deegans share my interest in plumb-stemmed, transom-sterned boats based on the Falmouth Quay punt, the working boat of Cornwall, so that type would set the tone of the design. Shallow draft, however, was a departure from the type, and it proved a challenge.

John and Dee wanted the layout to have a double berth, and provisions for two occasional guests. The bunks had to be well ventilated for the tropics. They only needed a single head with a cold-water shower draining to a sump, a hand basin, and a Lavac toilet. The U-shaped galley should have double sinks—one shallow, one deep—and plenty of counter space. For galley storage, they wanted a full-height cupboard as a pantry, and storage racks for china, cutlery, and glassware. A saltwater outlet and a whale foot pump from the freshwater tanks provide the water. Refrigeration is supplied by a 12-volt (Danfoss) refrigeration unit with a small freezer.

The rig is a masthead cutter with about 1,000 square feet in the working sails, set from a deck-stepped mast. There will be Profurl furlers on both headsails, a jiffy-reefed mainsail, and winches mounted at the foot of the mast. High bulwarks surround the deck, and an 8-foot dinghy with a sailing rig stows on the cabintop.

The engine is a Yanmar diesel, with Hurth gearbox, mounted in the midsection under a saloon table. A large, 60-amp "smart" regulator will top off the batteries. Fuel capacity will allow 800 to 1,000 miles of steaming. Ahead of the filters is a day tank for the fuel with a sight glass to monitor it for contamination. The prop shaft will be reversible, so it can be turned end-for-end as it wears. The propeller is a three-bladed feathering Max Prop.

Along with ventilation for the tropics, John asked for a diesel cabin heater for colder climes. Generous anchors and chain make up the ground tackle: a 60-pound CQR bower with 200 feet of chain and 150 feet of extra chain in the bilges; and a 30-pound CQR with 30 feet of chain and 150 feet of warp on the stern. A 12-volt anchor winch is on the foredeck. An Aries or Monitor windvane—or, better yet, a trim tab with a vane—and an electric autopilot attached to the trim tab will provide relief from hand steering.

I was worried—justifiably—about the shoal draft. The Falmouth Quay punts are known for deep draft. A 40-footer of that type may draw 7 feet or more. Of course, there would be a centerboard for lateral resistance, but I was concerned about having enough stability without the board. They wanted shoal draft to give them access to shallow water. The Great Barrier Reef, atolls in the South Pacific, estuaries like the Chesapeake and La Plata, and the Bahama Banks are all easier to navigate if draft is kept to a minimum.

The first step was a hull modeled in Maxsurf to see whether shallow draft could meet the stability requirements. Starting a new design in Maxsurf is a bit like making sourdough bread. I take an existing hull form from my files, type in new overall dimensions (length, beam, and depth of hull), and then "massage the net"—moving the control points that shape the hull's surface. Soon, a first draft is ready to analyze. The hull form then is exported to the Hydromax portion of the Maxsurf package, so I can run a full set of hydrostatic measurements.

The first-draft hull had 22,000 pounds of displacement. The dynamic stability factor assigns relative values to a series of parameters based on the dimensions, displacement, sail area, and stability. These can be compared with other boats along a range from sheltered sailing to inshore, offshore, and ocean sailing. This hull scored 90 out of 100; the cutoff for ocean sailing is 40. This provided some reassurance that we were on the right track. The displacement/length ratio came to 170, light by traditional standards. The sail area/displacement ratio of 22, based on the 1,000 square feet of sail area, is generous, as they wished. These figures all pointed to a boat that would meet their requirements.

Another important parameter in judging a boat's seaworthiness is the GZ, or stability curve, a graphic presentation of a hull's stability at various angles of heel. A boat gains in stability as it heels because its center of gravity and center of buoyancy are linked by a lever arm. As the heel angle increases, this lever arm increases to a point known as the maximum GZ. On this hull, that point is reached at 50 degrees of heel. If the boat continues to heel, the lever gets progressively shorter until a point of zero stability is reached. That was at 120 degrees of heel, 30 degrees past horizontal. Any further pressure puts the boat into a condition of negative stability until it's totally inverted.

It's important to design a hull that is not only stable upright, but also much less stable inverted. Comparing the volume under the curve in the positive and negative sides of the GZ curve graph, 85 percent of the volume is positive and only 15 percent is negative. Thus, the amount of energy required to unsettle the boat from its inverted con-

GZ Curve

dition is only a small percentage of what it takes to knock her over. This means that wave action in storm conditions that might lead to a capsize will be sufficient to re-right the boat.

It can be easy to lose sight of what all these numbers represent. We want to analyze the behavior of a proposed hull, so we turn to ratios and coefficients—static measurements. And of course a boat sailing is never in a static condition; all the parameters are constantly changing in reaction to the conditions the vessel is facing. Hydrostatics—whether laboriously figured by manual computation or arrayed in color on a computer screen—can do no more than provide "snapshots" of instants within a continuum.

The full analysis of a sailboat underway is about as complex as the analysis of a hurricane veering into the Caribbean. A model incorporating dynamic conditions can be created on a supercomputer, but without that kind of highly sophisticated Department of Defense hardware/software, no certainty can be found in any of these numbers—just footholds for one's intuition.

Computerization has changed the order in which I begin the development of a design. Traditionally, the starting points would be a sketch of the interior and a profile and sail plan. Due to the ease of establishing and measuring a hull form on the computer, I now start with a fully formed hull. Thus, right from the beginning, I can resolve basic questions about displacement and related coefficients. Now, when I begin work on an interior, I know the shape of the volume that contains it. This completely eliminates the chances of having a bunk that fits the deckline but ends up outside the hull due to the curvature of the sections. Later, if I need to adjust beam, draft, or length, it's easy to do.

As I began working up the design for the Deegans, I wrote them with some questions regarding the interior:

> How large a cockpit? Should it be aft, with tiller steering, or more amidship with an aft cabin and wheel steering? What amount of water would you like to carry? Since you have personal experience of your own water consumption, it seems silly to assign a value based on a rule of thumb. Last summer, you mentioned wanting to set up a rainwater retrieval system using the decks as the catchment. Any details you have already thought out would be very helpful.

I sent John and Dee a first draft and asked them to go over the plans and information and then mark any suggested changes on one copy of the blueprint and photocopies of the lines plan. It took a while, but finally their reply arrived, with an explanation for the delay:

> We have now left Sydney and are sailing up the east coast of Australia toward the Great Barrier Reef.... As you know, the preparations for a long trip are all-consuming....

We are now stuck in an anchorage on the northeast coast of Australia. I believe there is a post office up the river on the other shore— sure does not look like it, but we're going off in the dinghy to have a look. John put down his thoughts as a series of notes:

General Comments
- Although I would prefer tiller steering, I suspect that the boat is too heavy to steer with a tiller. Cable steering would probably be the next best bet.
- Fit a rubbing strip down the topsides; it makes docking easier and really helps the topsides.
- Dodger needs to collapse easily.
- Interior volume is important. For a boat to be a comfortable cruising boat, it needs to be a comfy home. I see in my mind's eye a chunky-beamy boat.
- I have changed the underwater profile a bit. Travelifts are rare out and about. The boat needs to sit easily on the hard.
- The cable shown from the back of the keel to the front of the skeg was a great success on *Innesfree* to deflect fish and lobster pots.
- The rudder as shown worries me. I suspect it will lose steerage, being so shallow. I realize this goes with the shoal draft. Why not a daggerboard to drop when required, especially on passage?
- Water catchment off the decks works well. Closed bulwarks with an exit each side works well with a system to block these off and open a valve on deck once the salt is rinsed away.
- Instead of scuppers, some boats have drains that lead to below the waterline, but this, I think, increases the underwater openings considerably.

First draft

Hull Aesthetics
- The coachhouse as drawn is quite intrusive. I would rather see one continuous line, with a deck-stepped mast. This style of coachhouse will increase headroom throughout, down below.
- The coachhouse, I think, can be brought back. The cockpit needs to have 6-foot cockpit seats, including the bridge deck, so that the crew can lie down outside.
- The freeboard looks way too low. I think that this can be increased considerably. This also will help the interior volume.
- Gallows as drawn would be a real head basher. Move it aft over the tiller or better over the dodger.
- Draft needs to be increased to about 4 feet. This looks too shallow. This should help your stability numbers.

Rig
- I would like to see a double-spreader rig.
- Plus masthead VHF antenna, anchor light, tricolor, Windex.
- Spinnaker running poles mounted on sliding tracks on the mast.
- We need a rig that allows a staysail with no running backstays.
- Sail area and proportions look just right to me. With an easy reefing system, the main should be easy to handle.
- Can the mainsheet and traveler be moved out of the cockpit? Maybe incorporated into the top of the gallows?

Engine
- A 40-hp Perkins 4108, in our experience, has a fuel efficiency of about 3 litres an hour (¾ U.S. gallon) at 5.5 knots. This works out to be about 100 gallons to cover 800 miles. Our present boat has a 73-hp Ford, and we get about ¾ gallon an hour at 6 knots.
- Move the engine under the cockpit so that the prop can be moved back to where I have sketched it.
- Fit a three-bladed Max Prop.

John's notes covered a great many points. Many were details that would be important eventually, but they were beyond the scope of what we needed to do at this point—to get the hull into a semblance of its final form. Then we could address the details. I worked up a second draft and sent it off with these comments:

Enclosed are the lines, sail plan, interior layout, and hydrostatics for the boat as I see it. The next time around, I'll be able to do an accurate stability calculation with a rollover test including the deck and house structures.

The throes of creation are sometimes laborious and messy. It's difficult to turn a few pages of information into a living, breathing boat without taking some liberties. You'll find I have not met your points one by one, although I hope I've met their spirit. My intention was not to present you with a "fait accompli" but to give you a starting point from which to lead me toward your goal.

The first draft of last winter was a bit of a false start. I was fighting against my instincts in a misguided attempt to give you what I thought you wanted. The result didn't satisfy either of us. I hope that by trying to satisfy myself, whenever your wishes were in doubt or obscure to me, the result will be more satisfactory.

We still have a moderately shoal boat, although the draft has been increased to 4 feet 6 inches. This may be deeper than you had hoped, but I find it hard to lessen the draft any more and still have a boat with the necessary headroom and stability range necessary for safety in any conditions—without resorting to a more contemporary hull type with extremely high freeboard and some sort of bulbed drop keel.

I've enclosed the sail plan and profile of a boat of the latter type that I'm designing for Jeff Halpern, a racer living in Annapolis, Maryland [see next chapter]. While the boat is to have offshore capabilities, it will be used primarily as a racer/cruiser in the Chesapeake and along the East Coast. If this is more like what you want, then I'm still on the wrong track!

The more moderate and traditional boat I've drawn for you would be a more wholesome home afloat, with easier motion and greater comfort. She should be fast over the long haul in cruising conditions, in part because greater comfort will make it easier to push hard without undue fatigue. All of this is a long-winded attempt to say that I hope that 4 feet 6 inches isn't too deep for you. If draft is still an issue, I'll try to lessen it in the next round.

I'm leery of using a daggerboard on the rudder of an oceangoing boat. It seems to be a complication just waiting to give trouble. Deepening the skeg and lengthening the rudder, as I've done, is a simpler solution. With a heavy skeg protecting the rudder and propeller,

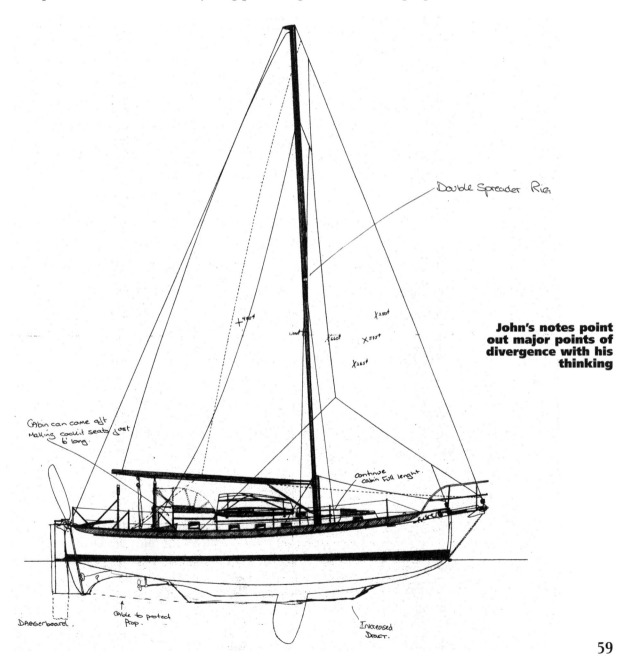

Double Spreader Rig

John's notes point out major points of divergence with his thinking

Cabin can come aft Making cockpit seats Just 6′ long.

Continue cabin full lenght.

DAEGerboard.

Cable to protect prop.

Increased Draft.

I don't think a cable across the keel cutaway gains anything. It would create drag far out of proportion to its apparent size, and would probably snag more weed than it would cut on this underbody.

The sail area has increased to 1,300 square feet. The rig is a bit taller. The main at 580 square feet is still under 600 square feet and should be easy enough to handle shorthanded. The rig has double spreaders, as you requested. I've run a shroud with some drift aft to the height of the staysail stay. This should allow you to fly the staysail without a runner. In heavy weather, a set of runners would be a good idea. They could be rigged at the height of the lower spreaders and support a storm jib flying from a "baby stay" at that height. Along with a storm trysail, that should give you a good way to snug the rig way down.

The dinghy is round-bottomed and strip-planked. It's based on the design I'm doing for Jenny Bennett [see Chapter 1]. Hers is 13 feet and intended as a dayboat. Yours is 9 feet long and, as you can see, will fit on the cabintop. The companionway slide now ships into a "hangar." The boom gallows straddles the cabintop and the main traveler is on the companionway hangar. The dodger is simplified.

I've rigged the spinnaker poles the way Lin and Larry Pardey carry them. They are attached at their upper ends and slide down tracks to reach working height, as opposed to being rigged from the lower end and raised to working height. This should keep them under more positive control, keeping the loose end low, where it's less likely to take charge.

Raised freeboard and the full-length cabin are definite improvements. That leads us down below. The engine has been moved aft. The companionway steps are in two stages, with a landing between. This leaves room for the engine and is more secure than a set of steep steps right down into the cabin. It should help keep the interior snug. At the foot of the steps are doorways into the head to starboard and the aft cabin to port.

The head has a wet locker reached from the cockpit through a hatch in the deck. It's near the engine, which will help dry things. There's room for a shower, and a counter with a basin, and lockers above and below.

You asked for sleeping accommodations for four people. I heartily agree with limiting the number of guests. By a strict accounting, this interior will sleep eight! In reality, this is only true in a marina. The forward cabin is the harbor cabin. It has a double berth, a hanging locker, and a seat. There's storage under the berth and in the built-in "bureau" forward of the hanging locker. There's a hatch above the sole to port of the berth for ventilation and safety.

The main saloon has a U-shaped banquette to starboard and a transom seat to port. Outboard of these is a pilot berth on each side, the sea berths for two guests. In a pinch, two more could sleep in the converted banquette (if you were to build it convertible); this is the kind of "roughing it" that should make it easy to get rid of extra company.

The aft cabin can be the harbor cabin for two guests and will be your sea berths. They're in a part of the hull with minimal motion, and near the cockpit and the nav station, but out of traffic. With a solid bundling board, as shown, between the two berths, they are snug for a seaway. In port, they can be converted to a double.

There's plenty of space for the galley. The sinks are on the centerline. The stove is gimbaled and provided with a crash bar. There are stanchions at the nav-seat back, the sink counter, and at the dining table. The one at the table carries the centerboard pendant up to the housetop, where it runs aft to within reach of the cockpit. It's a wide cabin—beam is 12 feet 3 inches. The stanchions and the banquette layout minimize the open spaces, where a body could pick up dangerous inertia lurching about in a seaway.

I should comment here that in these days of expansive interiors, it's often forgotten that all that space can be dangerous away from the marina. When it's important to be able to move from handhold to handhold, a wide-open cabin can turn a misstep into broken bones. But let's continue with the comments I sent to the Deegans:

The nav station is at the foot of the companionway to port. It's in direct communication with the cockpit but protected from wet by the long companionway passage. There's a bookshelf mounted transversely above the forward end of the table, with room for electronics under the side deck. I've drawn it with a side-facing seat; this makes it easier to stay put in a seaway and also maximizes the chart-table size. If you prefer fore-and-aft seating, the table can be L-shaped along the aft bulkhead and side, with the seat forward facing aft.

The galley has room for a large icebox under the counter aft, to be fitted with refrigeration gear as you outlined. The range is next. I've shown a four-burner with oven. All along the hull, there are lockers under the counter and above it. The sinks are in the counter forward. The round one is deep, the rectangular one shallow. A glass-and-china rack will fit over the sink counter.

There are three main hatches—the companionway, the skylight, and the fore-cabin hatch—and opening ports provide ventilation. Dorade vents can go in the aft cabin, the head, the galley, and the forward cabin. There's a kerosene heater at the forward bulkhead in the saloon.

There's storage under the seats, berths, and counters, as well as in the lockers. A chain locker is in the forepeak ahead of the watertight bulkhead. An anchor locker can be fitted on the foredeck. Under the cockpit is room for sail, line, and fender storage. A deck-box can be fitted on the forward end of the cabin, and another aft of the mast.

Tankage is mostly below the cabin sole. The settee and banquette seats can have tanks under them. I haven't worked them out in detail yet, but I feel confident there will be sufficient available volume. Batteries and engine spares fit under the bridge deck either side of a large hatch. The standing well can be fitted with a vise, and the deck edge is at a convenient height to use as a workbench.

My intention here has been to flesh out a starting point. I hope that, overall, we're on the right track. Looking over these drawings and notes in the cabin of your boat in some exotic harbor will offer a very different perspective from mine sitting here landlocked in front of a computer screen. I only wish I could have accompanied them, so I could be there now, talking you through them in person!

The Deegans were still in Australia, up in Cairns, when John responded:

> The design is looking great; we show it to all our yachtie friends and it gets all sorts of good comments.
>
> We are going to clear customs for Papua New Guinea about the second week in October. Now that our engine and gearbox are sorted out, it is time to get going. From PNG, we will go north to Micronesia, aiming to get to Guam around April next year. The seasons are tight, especially the typhoon season around Japan, where we hope to arrive early June. We have allowed two months in Japan, then we cross to the Aleutians and on to Alaska. If everything goes OK, we want to winter in Seattle the Christmas after next.
>
> I always do this underway, hence the messy writing. Sorry, but we are rolling downwind in the southeast trades:
>
> Hull and Rig
> • Lower the mast height by 5 or 6 feet and extend the bowsprit 4 or 5 feet. This, I think, will lower the center of effort, and not much sail area will be lost.
> • Try to incorporate a bow cockpit (i.e., Maurice Griffiths style). It keeps everything up there low, and the mud and stuff does not run along the deck, just out the drains. Being up in the bow, it does not take much room from below.
> • Centerboard. Can the pivot pin and the pendant be serviced while still afloat? Since Travelifts are rare where we cruise, I would like to be able to get at these.
> • Rudder. I would be happier with a shape as shown—I think that recent experience has found this setup better. What do you think?
> • What did you have in mind for steering? I would prefer a tiller, but would this be too heavy in a boat this size? If we go for a tiller, it must hinge up out of the way.
> • We are great fans of solar panels. Where would these fit in? Any ideas?
> • Back to the rudder. At extreme angles of heel (45 degrees)—ouch!— how much rudder remains immersed? I suspect not a lot. Please have a look at it.
> • The draft and underwater look OK to me.
> • Have you drawn runners in this rig? I would much prefer not to have them.

Second draft

- How about a large, sit-down chart table with ham radio, etc., above? I have indicated the area I mean.
- The back cabin is great. We would use this area for storage (i.e., sails, bikes, etc.) until the dreaded visitors are there; then we rearrange.
- With some thought, all the panels should be easily removable for access to engine and especially the stern gland.
- Dee likes the galley; needs a big hatch above.
- Chart table. Ninety percent of the time, this is the in-port office, and it has to be comfy and big.

The Deegans agreed to the increase in draft to 4 feet 6 inches, but John still campaigned for the cable across the aperture between the keel and skeg. I continued to disagree. It's the kind of thing that can be tried without needing to adjust the drawings. They agreed with the increase in sail area, and acknowledged that the runners would be useful for ocean crossings. I laid out the chart table more clearly in the next draft, since they hadn't understood my intention on the previous drawing. The head and the wet-locker storage were fine with them. They wanted a hatch over the galley, and a diesel heater instead of a kerosene one (as John had stated earlier). John was concerned about battery placement, wanting them as low as possible.

The next communication from the Deegans came from Woodlark Island in Papua New Guinea, after which they were heading for Palau

John's notes on the arrangement plan

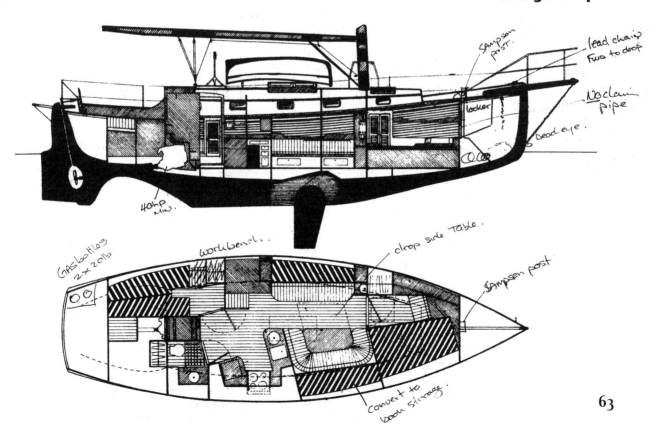

for a quick stop on their way north. While they were underway, I reviewed their comments and concerns about the design drawings, reconceived the interior, and sent them the new version with these comments:

The present layout takes advantage of the more centrally located engine, and a more developed aft cabin. The engine box is intersected by the aft cabin and head bulkheads. The top of the box is a seat at the foot of the companionway, useful as a perch for donning sea boots from the nearby hanging locker. This locker is reached from either the passageway or from the head, and it will keep wet gear out of the rest of the interior.

The nav station has an aft-facing swivel seat and is at the foot of the companionway for ease of communication. But it's sheltered from spray by the dodger and the fore-and-aft partition reaching to the forward end of the chart table. Instruments mounted on the partition are visible from the cockpit.

The pilot berths outboard of the saloon are sea berths, along with the aft-cabin double provided with lee cloths. The banquette can be used to sleep two more on that weekend-from-hell when everyone you know shows up and you can't send them off in the dinghy.

The forward cabin is still the master cabin in port, although the aft cabin is now a bit more spacious and has the advantage of greater comfort at sea. Ventilation and access are provided by ventilators over the galley and head, and skylights or hatches over the saloon and in the forward cabin. The aft-cabin berth has a portlight into the cockpit footwell for communication and cross-ventilation. The 12 ports in the cabin sides are large and opening.

The ground-tackle locker is in the foredeck and the chain locker is below it. Extra chain can be kept in the space under the forward berth and fed through a large conduit up to the windlass. The bitts are attached to the first collision bulkhead. The chain-locker bulkhead acts as a second collision bulkhead. (As you know, there's a lot of big junk out there to run into these days.)

Sail and lazarette storage are provided by two lockers to port in the cockpit. The forward one is accessible from the aft cabin. There's also a lazarette amidships to starboard. The propane locker is aft, to port.

The centerboard—1,400 pounds of steel and lead—is raised and lowered by a hydraulic winch and steel cable. Unfortunately, the pin is in the ballast keel and cannot be reached from on board. I am concerned with the forces involved here and the lack of a locking, fail-safe mechanism in case the cable were to part. The board flailing about in severe weather would be a great worry!

If there were a drop keel instead, its housing would be a partial partition between the banquette and the passage. It could be on a worm gear with hydraulic and manual systems for raising and lowering. In a worst-case scenario, it could be jettisoned. The loss of 13 to 15 percent of the ballast would not in itself be catastrophic, and it would be acceptable if the alternative were a ¾-ton battering ram loose aboard. Another advantage of the drop keel is that an end-plate/bulb can be used to lower the center of gravity and add to the lift of the foil.

This drop-keel idea has only just now come to me. The more I think about it, the happier I am with it as a superior solution. I don't want to make any major changes at this late date, but this is an alternative worth exploring. I've sketched some ideas in the margin. If you agree, I'll incorporate it into the final plans.

On to more pleasant subjects! The tender is based on Jenny Bennett's design for *Small*, shortened to 10 feet. Last weekend in Portland, I showed her your design and the tender, and she thought it could be called *Very Small*! This will be a real tender, capable of a large payload and provided with a sailing rig that can be hoisted with a halyard or dedicated tackle on the mast.

I've gone back to a trim-tab wind steerer, which should be easily rigged with the rudder configuration we now have. Enclosed is a perspective view of the boat on her beam ends, heeled to 45 degrees. This is in still water and, as you can see, there's plenty of meat still in the sea. With way on, the quarter wave will bury even more of the blade. I don't think this rudder will lose bite in broaching conditions.

The underbody has been reconfigured. The central engine location puts the prop farther forward, where it's less likely to break the surface in rough water. It's well protected by the rudder skeg, and although I haven't drawn it in, your "mine-sweeping" cable can be rigged from the keel to the skeg to protect it further. What about the arced strut I've penciled in? It will keep lines off the prop but doesn't provide a forward-facing corner to trap kelp, as a closed cable or strut would.

The rig is tall! It's right in the ballpark you specified for area. It'll fly tremendous light-air and tradewind sails, as well as stay above the lee of deep swells. As with the centerboard, the success of the rig will lie in the engineering of the mast. The challenge is to keep it light, strong, and relatively inexpensive. Either a tapered aluminum extrusion or a wood/composite spar is most likely to meet all three requirements. If a "stock" carbon-fiber spar could be found, it might be the best choice.

All in all, I'm very happy with the way the design is shaping up. Opinions at the boat show last weekend were also favorable. For someone less interested in maximum windward efficiency, I could see this boat rigged as a yawl-proportioned ketch with a double-headsail rig. You would beat them on slogs to windward, but a mizzen staysail would be a powerful addition off the wind, and the shorter main and second mast would bring greater peace of mind....

Now let me hit you with some figures: displacement 23,800 pounds; prismatic coefficient .52 pounds per inch; immersion 1,500 pounds; ballast 10,000 pounds; displacement/length 154; sail area/displacement 19.7; ballast/displacement .42 (not including full tanks in the bilge, chain, etc.); Dellenbaugh angle (10.75); wetted surface 466 square feet; sail area/wetted surface 2.2; total working sail 1,020 square feet; tradewind rig (genoa jib and genoa staysail set wing-and-wing) 1,094 square feet; light air to windward (main, genoa staysail, and jib) 1,106 square feet; light air off the wind (main genoa jib) 1,262 square feet.

Sails: main 512 square feet; genoa staysail 344 square feet; staysail 258 square feet; genoa jib (150%) 750 square feet; jib 250 square feet; trysail 90 square feet; storm jib (set to baby stay) 60 square feet.

That brought a quick short response from the Deegans, who were by then in Guam:

Thanks for sending the plans, they look great. We leave for Japan tomorrow, and I really do not have time to go over them and do your work justice. It should take two weeks to get to Japan, and with luck the weather will allow us to study them on passage.

A few weeks later, the next letter from the Deegans was still from Guam. They had decided to stay on for at least six months, probably a year, to work ashore and put money in their cruising account. John wrote:

I have marked several small changes but nothing of a major nature. The wheel steering as shown would be uncomfortable; I guess I would prefer a tiller, but this depends on the balance. In practical terms, we steer only on rare occasions, but it does need to be easy and, I also think, inviting.

Last week we had visitors on board for coffee; three of our guests had circumnavigated the world, one twice. The other two have cruised for at least 10 years each. I showed them your drawings and a very lively debate followed. Other than personal choice as to style, all agreed this would be a powerful, comfortable cruising boat.

I would call these the final drawings unless you decide otherwise.

At times, it was difficult getting feedback from people on a small boat half a world away, but I guess that's only within the context of what's possible in communications nowadays. On the whole, we were able to correspond well, and I'm pleased with the results.

This 40-footer combines traditional and contemporary elements. The choices have been based on a pragmatism without preconceptions. The tall rig provides good windward ability, but since most long-distance sailing is with the wind, this is a secondary benefit. A tall rig is blanketed less by large ocean swells, keeps the sails full, and lessens rolling, thereby reducing chafe.

The height of the rig adds to the transverse moment of the boat. It's counterintuitive, but this makes the boat less susceptible to capsize by a rogue wave. We think of capsize as the result of loss of stability; more stability should help resist capsize. That's true in normal conditions, but in a survival storm, rollover results from a combination of the extreme slope of an oncoming wave and the jet of high-speed water shot against a boat's side as the crest breaks. These forces are transitory, their effects lasting only seconds before passing on. In his book

Seaworthiness, the Forgotten Factor, Anthony Marchaj shows some
illuminating photos of tank tests illustrating this situation.

A boat with weights concentrated down low can be tripped quickly. That concentration raises the effectiveness of ballast in normal conditions. High weights, like the few extra pounds at the end of a tall rig, lessen stiffness in the normal sense but increase resistance to quick motions. Inertia at the end of a long lever arm, such as a mast, delays the boat's reaction long enough for the wave to pass. Think of the way a skater spins faster with arms retracted and slows down by spreading out her arms. By the time the boat starts to respond to the wave's force, the wave has passed—along with the crisis.

A more tender hull-and-rig combination is slower to respond to the steep side of a wave. It stays upright relative to plumb even when perpendicularity to the wave is a steep angle. A stiff hull would quickly roll perpendicular to the wave's steep side, carrying its center of gravity far out to leeward and adding to the danger of the jet of water from a breaking crest. A shoal hull is helpful in this regard. A deep keel grips deeper water below the surface disturbance of wave action. This gives the deeper keel an advantage in working to windward against wind and seas when they've blown long enough to send the surface flowing to leeward. The disadvantage arises when a boat on the face of a rogue wave is pushed bodily to leeward. If the keel digs in, it trips the boat, resulting in capsize. By combining a relatively shoal hull with a deep drop keel, we have the conventional advantages of windward ability and shoal draft for shallow waters, together with resistance to capsize from giant seas.

A cutaway underbody has low wetted surface. When combined with an efficient foil, it's weatherly and maneuverable. The drawback for the long-range cruiser comes from the loss of directional stability that often results. It's obvious that if a hull turns easily, it will require a lot of steering to maintain a course. A long underbody tracks like a locomotive, but it can be as hard to turn. Combining a long, shoal underbody with a deep foil and an aft-hung rudder should produce a boat that steers *and* tracks well.

Before we leave the Deegans' boat, I want to stress the importance of a long-range cruiser as a home afloat. That may be obvious, but the crux of it is that not only should it carry all the necessary supplies, and have the space to sleep, work, and relax, it also needs to *feel* like a home. Months at a stretch may pass aboard. The boat should have a variety of spaces above and below decks where the crew can find solitude when proximity gets wearing. Nor should anyone feel trapped in the cockpit; the whole deck needs to be inviting and safe. With this design, I've tried to meet all these requirements and create the seagoing home the Deegans envisioned.

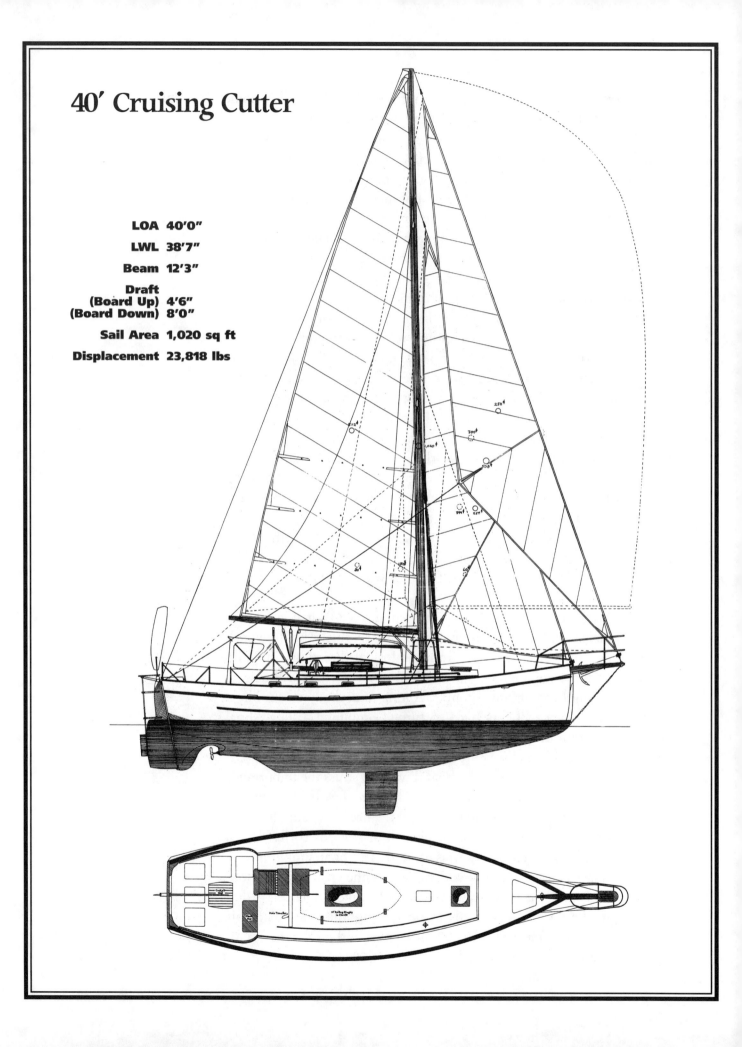

40' Cruising Cutter

LOA 40'0"

LWL 38'7"

Beam 12'3"

Draft
(Board Up) 4'6"
(Board Down) 8'0"

Sail Area 1,020 sq ft

Displacement 23,818 lbs

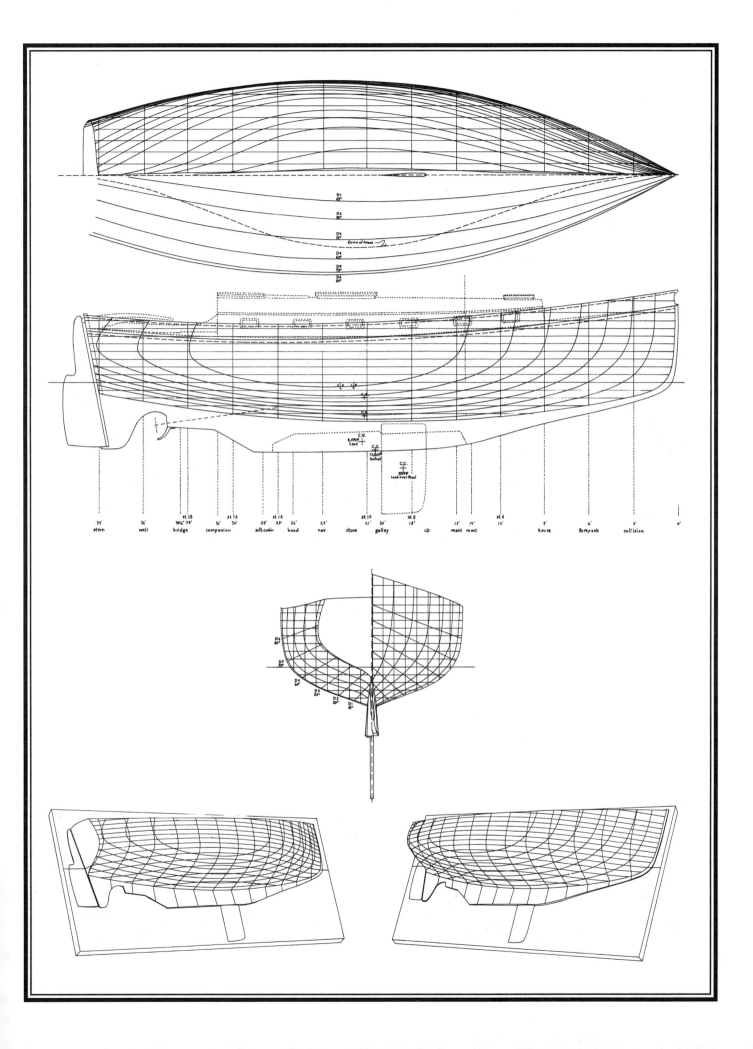

40' Cruising Cutter

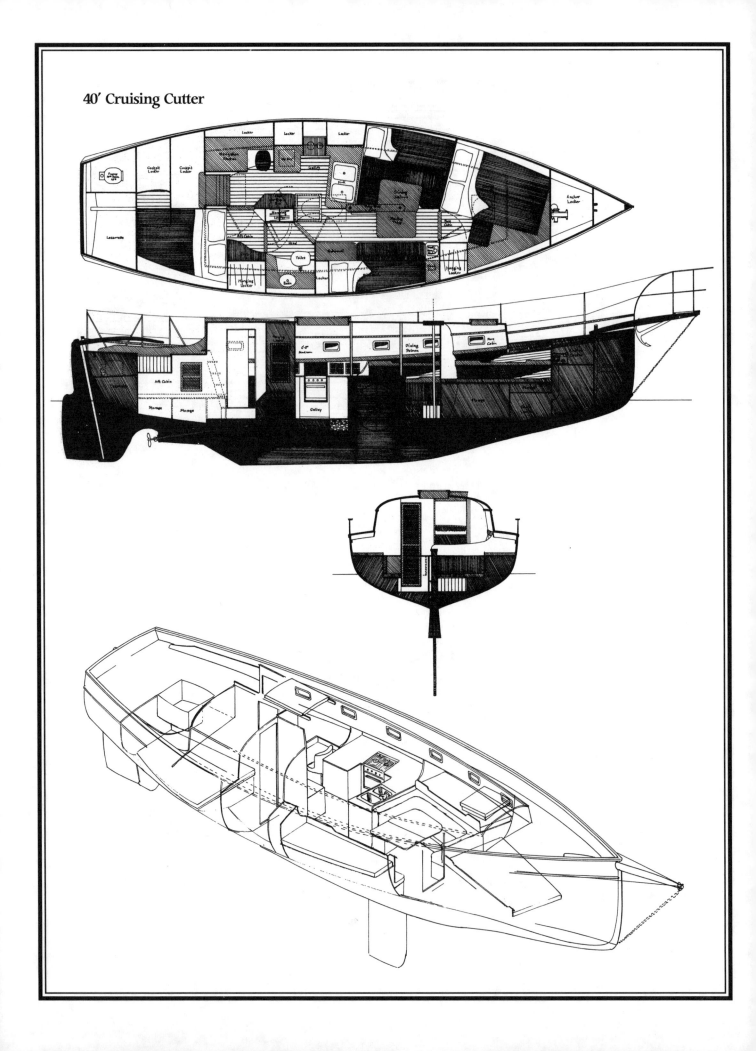

Chapter 4

Navy Point

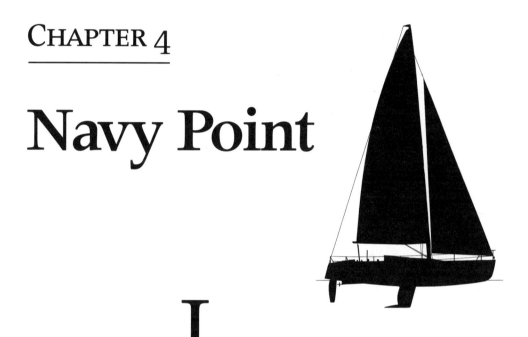

I met Jeff Halpern in 1991, at the Chesapeake Bay Maritime Museum's (St. Michaels, Maryland) Small Craft Meet. As we were getting ready to race our sailing canoe in the Saturday afternoon free-for-all, Jeff walked up. Before we knew it, he and I were in the same boat at the starting line. That year, we received an eighth overall out of a fleet of 30. Every year since then, we've raced my dinghy, *Harry*, or his sister, *Katrina*, garnering a first overall and a collection of wins and places in our class.

Jeff is a "dry land" architect, with his own practice, and an avid racing sailor. He's been active on the Annapolis, Maryland, racing circuit for years, and has had experience with traditional boats, having restored a Folkboat and a Stadel pilot sloop in his youth. For a time, he worked with noted naval architect Charles Wittholz. Now he sails a Laser 28, a Bruce Farr design, and extols the virtues of contemporary racing boats at every opportunity. Over the years, we've carried on a lively debate over traditional versus contemporary boats.

In 1995, we began collaborating on a cruising-boat design that would incorporate some of the features of the new "sport boats." We started with a 23- to 25-footer, Narwhal, and we've progressed to the

Designer & Client   Navy Point series—first a 31-footer and now the 44-footer. So far, these have just been "concept" boats, a way to give fuller dimension to our ideas.

Our discussions have revolved around the gap between traditional and contemporary sailors. Jeff's stance is that traditionalists are missing out on advances that make sailing easier, faster, and, in his opinion, safer. It's my contention that while some of this is true, the contemporary racer has narrowed the focus of sailing to efficiency alone. We both agree there's a rift between the two camps, with few points of commonality on which to base a dialogue.

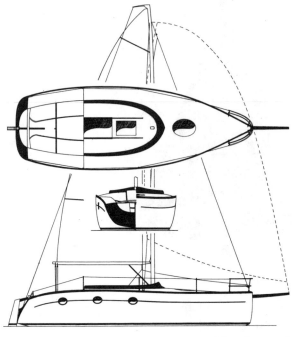

The start of the "sport boat" series

The development of Navy Point has been a sounding board for us. The design is problematic. While the other designs in this book may appeal to predominantly traditionalist readers, this one may leave them cold. A contemporary racer may only see the wooden hull, or concessions to cruising, and condemn the boat as well. In the end, the boat may not satisfy Jeff or me, either. Despite all of that, I think the exercise has been valuable, and the questions raised worthy of being aired.

Jeff was concerned that my work might be pigeonholed, and he felt that the inclusion of this design would broaden the scope of my work. For myself, even though I have a predisposition for traditional boats, and most of my work is based on traditional types, I'm not unmoved by the excitement of contemporary sail. I hope to be open to relevant technology in all the boats I draw.

Jeff feels that the wooden-boat world is too parochial, and cut off from the wider realm of contemporary boating:

> [While] much of...[contemporary sailing] is frivolous and without...clear merit, integrity, or aesthetic value...much of it represents good thinking and a genuine advance in the art and science of yacht design. These breakthroughs yield boats that are more than fast. They are easy to handle shorthanded, gentle on crews and rigs, seaworthy, and, most of all, able to sail—and sail well—in a much broader range of conditions than the boats of the past.... The wooden-boat world is distancing itself from the possibility that wooden boats will become a major factor for mainstream yachting.

Jeff's brief for a contemporary cruiser/racer features the points he finds worth emulating:

> I would like a 43- to 45-foot fractional-rigged sloop.... She could be owner-built. I intend to own her for a long period of time. Initially

she would be fitted out rather minimally and used for daysailing, coastal cruising, and incidental racing. Over time, as money is available and my sailing goals change, she will be upgraded—with the eventual long-term goal of prolonged offshore passages and life aboard as a retiree.

She is intended as [neither] a round-the-world cruiser nor a floating hotel. Sailing ability, maneuverability, and convenient sailhandling equipment are high priority. Varnish and a sumptuous interior are low priority.

Efficient foils.... Since she will be sailed on the Chesapeake and later on the southeast coast and the Caribbean, I would like her to have a daggerboard keel with a bulb and a shaft-hung spade rudder. With the board fully down, I would like about 8 feet of draft, and, with the board up, approximately 5 feet.

To increase stability on long passages...a water-ballast system similar to that used on OSTAR and Whitbread boats.

Jeff went on to provide a list of particulars:

LOA: 44 ft. 0 in. to 45 ft. 0 in.
DWL
  Half load: 38 ft. 6 in.
  Full load: 39 ft. 0 in.
Draft
  Board up: 5 ft.— 6 ft. max.
  Board down: 8 ft. 0 in.
Displacement
  Half load: 15,000 lb.
    (w/o ballast water)
  Full load: 18,000 lb. max.
    (w/o ballast water)
Sail area
  Main: 600square ft.
  Jib (100%):   460square ft.

Capacities:
  Potable water
    Fixed tanks: 60 gal.
  Bladders: 60 gal.
  Fuel-Diesel: 50 gal.
  Alcohol: 5 gal.
  Ballast water: 1,200 lb. per side

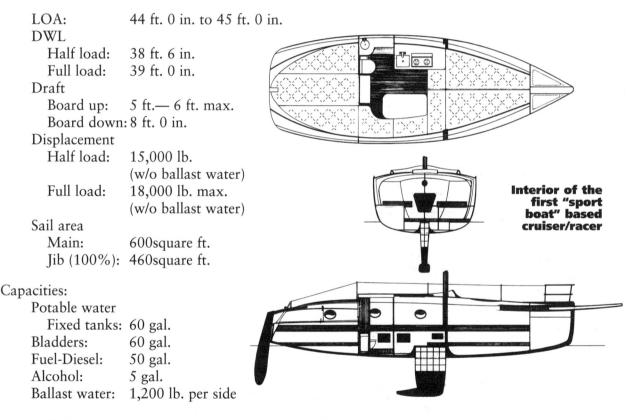

Interior of the first "sport boat" based cruiser/racer

Jeff's list of particulars continued with a detailed walk-through of the boat, starting at the bow. There should be a low flush foredeck free of obstacles, two bow rollers, an anchor locker with a windlass under the deck, a chain locker under the forepeak, and a hatch in the deck for ventilation and sail stowage. The cabinhouse should be low, with opening portlights. The running rigging is sent aft over the housetop to deck organizers with line clutches. Jeff's list of lines is formidable: "two wing spinnaker halyards, two wing jib halyards, a main halyard, a Cunningham hauler (doubles as first reef tack line), two reef tack lines, the outhaul, three reef clewlines, double-ended vang (one end per side), inboard pole lift, inboard pole downhaul, outboard pole lift, port spinnaker-pole gybing line, starboard pole gybing line, and the centerboard pendant." (And modern sailors complain about gaff cutters having too many strings....)

Jeff felt that the cockpit should be "long enough and laid out so that a person can easily and comfortably sleep...." A dodger will "form a kind of open pilothouse" over the companionway. He acknowledged that steering probably would have to be by wheel, although he prefers a tiller. The suggestions continued:

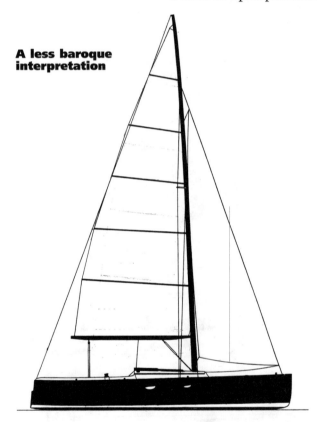

A less baroque interpretation

> The jib tracks should be full-length Harken roller track with lead adjusting tackles. The spinnaker sheets should run through an adjustable twing system. Both the jib and the spinnaker sheets should run through turning blocks before the primary winches. The primary winches should be motorized and placed on winch islands that permit cross-sheeting. All sheets should be led to the winches through stops.
>
> The mainsheet should be controlled from a cross-cockpit traveler with control lines within easy reach of the wheel. The mainsheet should be a continuous loop led to self-tailing winches on either side of the boat forward of the wheel. Adjacent to the traveler should be a control panel with the backstay adjuster and a mainsheet fine-tune.

Along with light displacement and tall sail plans, sail controls such as these are the heart of what makes the contemporary racer perform as it does. They may seem bewildering to someone more familiar with a snotter than an adjustable backstay, but with sophisticated control over mast bend, sheeting angles, and sail shape, a boat can be sailed very efficiently. In light air, the rig can be powered up with a deeper camber to the sails; in heavy air, the sails can be flattened to reduce heeling force. Reefing can be delayed, and when the time comes, it can be done "on the fly" in a few moments. The infinitely adjustable rig, coupled with light displacement, means the sail plan is smaller than would be necessary on a heavier boat. All this means that the loads and the gear can be lighter as well.

Jeff also urged that "There should be ample coamings that slope to the exterior to permit proper 'fanny lock.'" This is an example of another real breakthrough in contemporary design: ergonomic layout. Contemporary cockpits have been laid out to optimize crew comfort and efficiency of handling. On the other hand, a traditional cockpit can be comparatively awkward, since layout is based on the structural requirements of traditional construction, rather than on the best way to seat the crew.

Jeff provided more comments about deck layout:

> There should be a small cabin trunk at the aft end of the coamings. The sides of the coamings will form the cabin sides and the cabintop will have a moderate crown and a forward-facing companionway. If possible, there should be a small afterdeck to facilitate line handling.

Jeff then turned to the particulars of the layout below decks. Starting forward, there will be a collision compartment with a watertight bulkhead. Nowadays, the abundance of large floating debris, combined with speeds nearing 20 knots, make this no idle concern. Closing off the compartment in the bow overhang behind a watertight bulkhead also keeps weight out of the bow, where it has such an adverse effect.

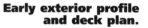

Early exterior profile and deck plan.

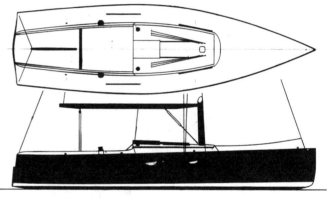

The forward cabin has two pipe berths with "canvas lockers," a series of pouches hanging on the inner hull that provide inexpensive, flexible, lightweight storage. Below the berths are workbenches and lockers for tools and spare parts. The storage system incorporates handy "milk-crate" bins in racks. They can be loaded at home, brought aboard, and slipped into their racks.

The mast is deck-stepped, and a compression post carries the loads down to the keel. The daggerboard trunk is aft of that. More milk-crate storage racks fit into lockers in the passageway. Water-tank bladders fit below the lockers. There's a head aft of the forward cabin with a lavatory, toilet, and shower. In the main cabin are a pair of transom berths with pilot berths outboard. The U-shaped galley counter is to starboard. Across from the galley is a head leading to a passageway to the aft cabin. The nav station is aft of the galley to starboard. A sail locker fits under the side of the cockpit with access from above. The engine is under the cockpit floor and is accessible from the aft cabin and the passageway.

The boat is built with a strip-planked wooden hull sheathed inside and out with biaxial fiberglass cloth saturated in epoxy. Integral bulkheads provide the framework for the hull and give it transverse strength. The bulkheads are of high-density foam sandwiched between marine-plywood skins. The floors, keel, and ring frame at the mast are all laminated wood. The spars are aluminum and the spinnaker pole is carbon fiber. The daggerboard is fabricated with a galvanized-steel framework sheathed in foam and fiberglass saturated in epoxy. The bulb is cast lead bolted to the framework.

During the winter of 1995, the Atlantic City [New Jersey] Boat Show sharpened my perception of the need for boats that were neither all-out racers nor floating cocktail lounges. Strip composite construction and a break with traditional forms opened up possibilities for the way a boat could look. I found it limiting to see the choices reduced to the narrow visions touted at the show as "state-of-the-art." The racers all have a stripped-down aesthetic, going on the assumption that form follows function. The party boats follow an aesthetic based on the most crass fashions in interior decoration. My reaction to each style was, "Is that all there is?"

Early accommodation plan.

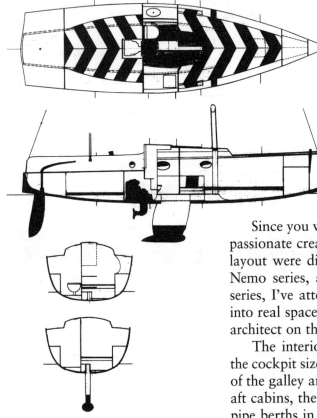

After I returned home, I sent off some initial drawings to Jeff of the Navy Point 44 and pointed out that the project suffered a bit from space inflation in the arrangement. When it came time to shoehorn everything into the available space, some things had to give. (Jeff recently admitted that the shortest length into which he could fit his original specifications was 53 feet.)

When I sent Jeff the drawings, I outlined the situation:

Since you wrote your original specifications in the "white heat of passionate creation," your sense of size and proportions within the layout were distorted. My wife, Kay, calls these boats my Captain Nemo series, and since I didn't want to start on a Salvador Dali series, I've attempted to translate your requests from dream space into real space. Naturally, I'm relishing this opportunity to chide an architect on this most basic human failing!

The interior has developed around the daggerboard trunk and the cockpit size and location. The first naturally led to the placement of the galley and banquette, and the latter to the arrangement of the aft cabins, the head, and the storage/passageway. While I've shown pipe berths in the forepeak per your instructions, I would prefer to see them superseded by the additional port aft cabin, with the forepeak dedicated to sail storage and the second head. I would lengthen the collision compartment aft by another foot to incorporate the chain pipe and lighten up the bow still further.

Otherwise, I think I've met the general trend of your requests. Lazarette storage is limited. There are two shallow cockpit seat lockers to port, and a hatch to the starboard passageway. Stores can be passed through the hatch instead of carried down the companionway and aft through the head. Part of the storage space to starboard of the aft cabin could have access from boarding steps at the transom. This could incorporate a fuel locker for the damned inflatable.

Storage below for your modular milk crates is consolidated in the passageway. There is a substantial locker space outboard, and another along the centerline above the main fuel and water tanks. I would concentrate heavy gear, like a toolbox and heavy stores, in this 'midship location, where it has the least detrimental effect on the boat's trim and pitching moment.

I was reluctant to accommodate the request for water-ballast tanks, the sort of monkeywrench I find very hard to accept. Not only does it add another complicated system to the boat, but it's a feature upon which the safety of the craft depends. To some extent, I have come around and compromised. For the "sled" type of hull used on Navy Point, I agree that some form of water ballast is necessary to keep the boat in proper fore-and-aft trim as she heels. The long knife bow, coupled with relatively flat quarters, tends to trim bow down even at low angles of heel. In a dinghy, this is counteracted by flying the crew on their trapezes right off the weather quarter. When the same hull form is used in larger craft, the trimming must be done with movable ballast.

My explanations continued:

The engine shown is a Yanmar 3-cylinder sail drive. These are available in 18-, 26-, and 32-hp (continuous rating) models. The rig is tall. Most of the boats in this size range nowadays tend to have slightly smaller rigs of about 800 square feet. The all-out racers among them have lighter displacements to match. The boat can certainly stand to this tall rig. It's more a question of bridge clearance and expense of the mast and rigging that would compel us to dock the spar.

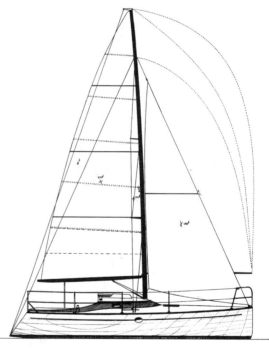

Third generation of smaller "sport boat"-derived cruiser/racer

I hope you don't find the profile too "arty" for your taste. I do have definite ideas on how I would like to style the exterior. I think the aft cabin is a great opportunity to quote from the "boat stern" used in speed launches and automobiles in the 1930s. The cabin and cockpit coaming should follow the current standards and blend into the deck, for both safety and comfort. There is an opportunity to clear-coat epoxy and varnish the coaming, house sides, and the topside "wale." Or they can be painted a contrasting color.

I am excited by the lines. I've tried to follow a moderate course here. The boat is long and relatively lean with 12-foot beam. The turn of the bilge is slack; that tremendous bulb is doing most of the righting work. The long entry should please you and slice nicely through waves. The run is long, and little affected by changes in load line or trim.

The pounds-per-inch-immersion is almost 1,400. Running the boat stripped out at a savings of 2,000 pounds displacement will change trim less than an inch and a half. The prismatic coefficient is about optimum at .53. It's hard to get enough fullness with that long snout. The U-shaped forward sections and the long midbody help.

For now, this just provides a baseline, from which we can battle on to a final design. It's a hybrid in a number of respects. First, it's a custom wooden boat in the model of a production fiberglass boat. Second, it's a cruiser, and potential live-aboard with pretensions as a racer. It's also, coming from my perspective, a combination of traditional elements with biomorphic shapes.

I came of age in a period when contemporary design was in a horrible decadence. It was easy for those of us drawn to wooden boats in the 1970s to ignore most of what was going on in the larger market. I'm afraid it's a mistake to continue that prejudice today. There is a cultural chasm between the separate worlds. There are also differences in temperament between the highly commercial and competitive contemporary sailors and the more contemplative and communitarian members of the traditionalist camp. Both sides bring prejudice and lack of knowledge about the other to their opinions. It's hard to take individual ideas and judge them on their merits instead of as just symbols of the other camp's loyalties.

I don't see this design as *the* great synthesis of the two worlds. It's weighted too far toward the contemporary side. You'll probably see it as too far weighted in the other direction, perhaps as too "weighty," as well.

During this period, I joined the Society of Boat and Yacht Designers' newly established Chesapeake branch, so Jeff and I had more frequent opportunities to meet and hash out our ideas. We also found time to sail *Rugosa*, Jeff's Laser 28. Nothing brings the subjectivity of sailing into greater focus for me than these outings on Jeff's boat. He describes the boat's performance as exhilarating and full of nuanced control. My own perceptions were of a boat that sailed at a high angle of heel and whose narrow-bladed rudder stalled out easily with the slightest overcorrection to weather helm in the puffs. The heel angle was exacerbated by the beaminess of the boat aft. When taken up in a gust, we were standing on the lee cockpit seat edge, with the water some 7 feet below us. You could hear the air sucking down the lee face of the blade as we rounded up until control was regained.

I know I'm not fair to the totality of the "sport boat" to focus on my discomforts during what were only short introductory sails. All thoroughbreds are temperamental, and it takes time, and an overriding appreciation for their speed, to learn what they're like. We passed every boat in sight on those outings...well, maybe not the cigarette boats.

I bring up my reservations to show the source of some of our disagreements. It's not to say that my response was more valid than his. The different values we place on elements of a boat's performance seem to affect the way we perceive the results. A racer is always willing to put up with idiosyncrasies if they bring the reward of increased speed. My cruising sensibility sees speed as only one aspect of a well-rounded boat.

There's no question that it should be possible to design boats that combine good turns of speed with good general behavior. This can be achieved only by compromising from both sides. The edge of the true racer must be toned down, and the sleepy stolidity of an all-out cruiser must be sharpened.

It's too bad that races can be judged only by speed. Comfort should be reflected in the stamina a crew can bring to the course, but that is usually overcome by stoicism and athletic training. Winning crews may be sailing the least comfortable boats and still come out ahead. Perhaps the cruiser should keep to the internal rewards of his pursuit, and leave the silver to the racer pitting herself against others in an outward contest.

The next version of the plans showed a refinement of the hull, and I sent along an explanation to Jeff:

> The biggest changes are in the hull lines: the added flare amidships and the flattened run. The rudder is a bit higher aspect, also. The most drastic change might be the abandonment of the lifting keel in favor of a conventional one. Besides the complication of the mechanism required, the rake of the foil and a bit more area have led me to the present configuration. The bulb is 4,000 pounds of lead; water ballast is 1,200 pounds per side. (The foil in the body-plan view is only half; that's why it appears so thin.) The rudder is longer and has moved forward over earlier versions. This is to delay aeration.

A foil, like a wing, achieves lift by creating a pressure differential from side to side. The difference between a foil and a wing is that a foil is working at or near the boundary between the fluid in which it operates (water) and a much lighter one (air). A high-aspect foil, like a modern, deep, narrow rudder, generates a lot of lift as a result of the high pressure differential it develops from side to side. If there's no barrier at the surface of the water, there's a tendency to draw air down the low-pressure side. This is called aeration, and it destroys lift and causes the foil to stall. (That's what Jeff's Laser 28 was doing on our gusty outing.)

Aeration is rarely a problem for keels. The hull acts as an effective barrier to aeration, although it's still possible at high angles of heel. An effective rudder must be as far aft as possible, where it has the most leverage in turning; yet it has to be far enough under the hull to reduce the chances of aeration.

Outboard motors have a similar problem that's dealt with by placing a cavitation plate above the propeller. This keeps air from being drawn down into the prop. (The term *cavitation* actually is misused in this regard. It means the vaporization of water in extremely low-pressure areas at the tips of high-speed propellers—an explosive decompression that may damage the blades.) Some transom-hung rudders on high-performance sailboats have used endplates at the surface for the same reason. Some endplates are on the bottom of rudders, to prevent a similar, but less dramatic, loss of pressure across the tip from the high-pressure side to the low.

An early configuration of the Navy Point

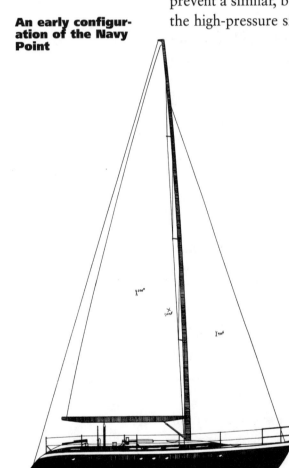

The problem with endplates, top or bottom, is pitching. As a boat pitches and heaves in a seaway, the rudder is at times moving across the direction of flow; it's rarely in a consistently horizontal path. Endplates are alternately functioning normally, channeling the flow, and also acting as brakes, creating turbulence and eddies as they charge up and down. Since the hull is an essential structure, you're not going anywhere without it. It makes sense to use it to block aeration instead of introducing more wetted surface and eddy-producing protuberances.

The latest rudders of this type are now often within inches of the depth of the keel. I see the need for high-aspect ratios, and the added length might delay aeration a bit further, but I don't think it's wise to expose a fragile rudder to such a grounding hazard.

When an element is developed that offers an increase in speed to a racer, it is retained regardless of other drawbacks. In the case of a high-aspect rudder, inherent weakness and vulnerability are addressed by strengthening the rudder stock and bearing. Aeration is dealt with by placing the rudder under the hull, and by lengthening it almost to the depth of the keel. These are, from my perspective, contingent solutions. They don't solve the problems, only mitigate their consequences. A racer is excited by the thrill of eking out advantages by accumulating such devices. The cruiser's inherent conservatism lends itself to redundancies of safety and economy. We look for a rudder, or keel, that is efficient as a foil yet with a shape and position that contribute to a soundness of structure and ease of use.

So my explanation to Jeff continued:

> A large problem in adapting the contemporary racer type to cruising is in the vulnerability of the foils. A compromise should be reached between the benefits in speed and weatherliness of this underbody and its vulnerability—especially if the boat is to be in any measure an economical cruiser. The deep draft, the high strain, the susceptibility to entanglement, the difficulties of beaching, and the awkwardness in a serious grounding are all factors that mitigate against the type.
>
> The hull has been refined. I've endeavored to fine the entry, moderate the beam aft a bit, carry the flare amidships to put the water ballast as far outboard as possible, and cut away the bow. The transom shows reverse rake, which I hope is slight enough not to interfere with stern-to docking. I do think that boarding steps built into the transom would be a good idea. The other alternative is a boarding/swimming ladder, but this will definitely be in the way and prone to damage.
>
> The center-cockpit arrangement is the best utilization of the space available. The aft cabin is enormous; there is plenty of space for the engine, and tankage and storage below the cockpit, at the center of buoyancy. The head, galley, and nav station are near the companionway. The saloon extends from the forward keel bulkhead to the one ahead of the ring frame, and then to the forward cabin.

Based on my lessons from Navy Point, a wheelhouse layout would be best from a cruiser's perspective. The center of the boat is opened upward for the most spacious interior. The cockpit moves aft. It would be smaller perhaps with an aft cabin, although that might best be left for a longer version. I'm interested in developing a wheelhouse layout with a more balanced hull and less vulnerable foils. It will be more of a fast cruiser, with oceangoing potential intended for a shorthanded crew. A ketch rig with the masts well separated for better windward ability, and the potential for large mizzen stays'ls, might work well, too.

Enough speculation; back to my comments to Jeff on the Navy Point design:

> If we can settle on the major points, I'll work up the interior for the boat as it now stands. I understand it should be simple and spacious, laid out for two with occasional guests.
>
> A word on the hull and deck shapes and their suitability for strip/composite construction. There's nothing in the shape of this boat that is prohibitive for strip building. In fact, the curvatures add strength to the structure. The contours of the deck and house offer no problems. The cockpit coamings are planar and will be laminated into a box structure.

Jeff responded with his usual level of detailed critique:

Designer & Client

I really like the direction that the design is moving in. I still have some minor concerns about the hull shape. I feel that the waterline beam has gotten a bit too wide, especially at the transom. I think that the point of maximum beam at the waterline could be moved as far forward as the forward cockpit bulkhead, with the waterline beam reducing from there. This would allow slightly more flare in the after topsides and a slightly less flat section in the run. I also think that the sheer should be higher at the forward end of the boat to avoid that droopy-snout look that sometimes occurs on modern boats.... The sheer should be raised from...the aft end of the cabin all the way to the stern.... The stem can be as much as 6 inches higher than in your drawing.... I have serious reservations about building a fixed-keel boat that draws 8 feet, but I am not sure we should go back to the daggerboard idea.

Three cabin/center cockpit layout

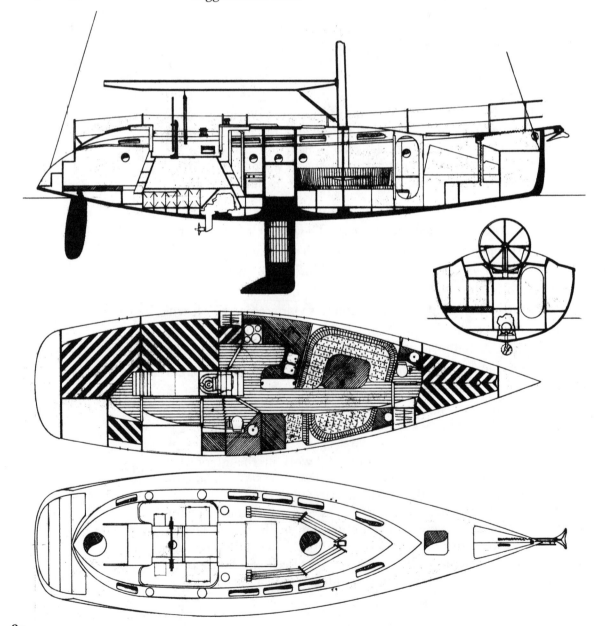

I have a number of minor concerns:

- The cockpit is so far forward that the main cabin is occurring in the narrowest part of the boat. I would really like to have pilot berths in the main cabin, and if the boat is too narrow, this would be a problem.
- The aft cabin makes it difficult to lay out proper mainsheet and traveler controls.
- Four-thousand pounds sounds too light for the fixed ballast. Since shifting water ballast takes awhile (20 to 30 seconds), the boat needs adequate ballast to stand to its rig. When you calculated the ballast weight, did you include anything for the keel foil? If you didn't and we are not doing a lifting keel, perhaps the foil could be cast iron or lead.
- I have a pet peeve about ports in the hull forward of the chainplates. In fact, I really don't like ports in the hull at all. The caulk joint is exposed to all kinds of stress and wave action, and frankly, they are hard to reach to maintain. (I hate dropping tools over the side.) Remember, here in the Chesapeake, we don't haul our boats for the winter.
- The forward face of the house should be a flatter angle so that one can get good footing while working at the front of the mast.
- Needless to say, I do not share your concerns about fin keels. As to the grounding issue, it is only an issue of biblical scale to those ensconced in traditional boat thinking. It does not seem to be an issue in real life. While there have been notable keel and rudder failures, this is not the norm. There have also been notable hard groundings survived by fin-keelers. Trust me, I was aboard when one hit a rock quite hard and mushroomed the lead, but that was all. Seriously, it will be crucial to engineer the keel and rudder for a grounding, but this is not an out-and-out raceboat, so this is one area of the boat where additional weight will not hurt a thing. From my past experience, I would rather get my Laser 28 off the hard than my old Stadel cutter.

I look at highly stressed appendages like the keel and rudder of this type and cringe. Certainly they can and do work. That doesn't change my perception of their vulnerability. Is my attitude like that of the World War I pilot complaining that new planes don't have struts and cables to hold the wings on? I don't think it's that simple. It comes down to a fundamental difference of approach. These new boats grow out of a design philosophy in the mainstream of contemporary technological thinking. The design problem is broken down into discrete questions. Each question is broken down into its basic components. These are analyzed numerically, and solutions are decided upon. The boat is an assemblage of discrete units.

It's not that the boat is a Frankenstein creature with staples and sutures showing. A strategy integrates the parts, reflecting the basic tenets of the philosophy: light weight is good, high loadings on sails and foils are good, low wetted surface is good, maneuverability and adjustability are good. Complexity of engineering and systems is to be embraced. The high cost of complex components and questions of their reliability are to be tolerated. Supporters of modern design see these assumptions as self-evident and in no need of review. To them, a faster, lighter, livelier boat is the only kind worth considering.

My own perspective is at odds with a purely technological view of design. I can't give such primacy to what I see as one of many possible sets of criteria for a successful design. Design is a resolution of human desires, not the fulfillment of a particular set of performance parameters. I don't find any particular parameters to be paramount— beyond safety and a level of economy.

So let's go back to the rudder and keel. The most efficient foil for creating lift, whether for steering force or to counteract leeway, is a long, thin blade without obstructions. The rudder is partially balanced, meaning the pivot is behind the leading edge. The shaft is made brutally strong, with stainless steel and carbon fiber in the highly stressed components. This is necessary because the rudder is only attached at its root, like the elevons on a fighter jet's tail. The keel is also a narrow foil blade attached to the hull by one thin edge. From it hangs a large bulb of lead. The enormous stresses can be carried by well-engineered, super-strong materials. The analogy to modern aircraft holds. Many of the structural solutions are the same for boats as for aircraft.

Planes require a level of technical support that shouldn't be necessary with boats, and of course the aerial environment is different from the marine environment in significant ways. Let's look at the first point. There is an inherent rigor to flying. No plane can afford to have a failure that compromises its ability to perform. If it can't fly, it crashes. For this reason, it has always been accepted that engineering and maintenance must both be carried out to the highest possible standard. Judged by the alternatives, the expense required is not debatable.

It is true that a boat will fail its crew catastrophically by sinking, but sinking is the result of a loss of physical integrity, not a loss of function. A boat will float, and can protect its crew satisfactorily, even if it can't move at all under its own power. In this respect, it's more like a blimp than a fighter aircraft. Continually upping the stakes on engineering and maintenance doesn't have the same fundamental rationale in a pleasure craft. That's not to say that certain boaters may not be fascinated by playing with these issues. It's their money, their game.

When I say there are significant differences between the marine and aerial environments, I don't mean the differences in fluid properties expressed in theoretical aero- and hydrodynamics: density, compressibility, etc. The marine environment is full of obstructions. There are floats and lines from lobster pots, streamers of kelp, and plastic garbage—all waiting to entangle. There's also the bottom.

A committed racer has to set his priorities with little regard for the consequences, or he risks losing out to his more daring competitors. Viewing ports are needed ahead of appendages to monitor entanglements, and a crew member occasionally may have to climb over the side to free the underbody of debris. All part of the game. Jeff's protestations regarding the lack of danger in grounding a boat on the high heels of a fin keel may be due to the small tidal range and soft bottoms of the Chesapeake. I cannot ignore the images in my mind's eye of the results of such a grounding where tides are high and the bottom jagged. The racer has little room to complain, so long as competition is the ruling concern.

Lest I come off as a complete troglodyte, let me add that it's the attitude toward the use of technology I object to, not the techniques themselves. I disagree with the assumptions. Light displacement isn't the only way to achieve adequate speed. For some usages, a light, lively hull is just not comfortable enough for pleasure or safety outside the discipline of racing. Going out on technological limbs is not always worthwhile, unless self-sufficiency, cost, and maintenance are taken into account. Finally, fast sailing wasn't invented yesterday; there have been fast boats in the past, and they have always been the result of compromising other features to achieve speed. This equation has not fundamentally changed.

After attending a Society of Naval Architects and Marine Engineers (SNAME) meeting in January 1997, Jeff sent me a report:

> The SNAME symposium was very intense. Much of the time I was clearly over my head. Several of the presentations were relevant to our project....
>
> As a yacht-designer groupie, I was really enjoying myself. Present were people from Bruce Farr's office, S&S [Sparkman & Stephens], McCurdy & Rhodes, the Glen L. Martin wind tunnel, the Delft [Holland] and Southampton [England] testing facilities, Mystic Seaport, Kaufman and Associates, and many more.... Some of the well-known individuals included Olin Stephens, Jerry Milgram, Bruce Farr, Jay Paris, John Marshall, George Hazen, Charlie Morgan, Jay Benford....
>
> I sat with Ian McCurdy of McCurdy & Rhodes, who graciously answered my dumb questions. He had some very interesting thoughts on the design of performance cruisers. His work tends to be a bit more moderate than radical. He seems to be an advocate for keeping seaworthiness with comfortable motion a factor—an important factor—in the safety of the vessel. He indirectly made the case that the crew of a moderate design would not be thrown around and (not prone to) the more violent accelerations experienced on the current breed of light racers.... The crew of a moderate design would be more rested and therefore in better shape to deal safely with any con-

tingency that might arise. I sometimes forget that I have not spent any serious time at sea.

He also seemed to dismiss the idea of water ballast for general use. He felt that the systems were too slow and complicated for use in general coastal sailing. I would have loved to ask Bruce Farr for his thoughts on this, since he designed the water-ballast systems for the Whitbread boats.

There was a lot of discussion about the Vendee Globe tragedies. [This was the 1996 round-the-world race in which three boats capsized and one sailor was killed.] Boats had gear failure and encountered basic seaworthiness issues. During the symposium, there was a photo circulating showing one of the Vendee Globe boats turned turtle with its keel and bulb pointed skyward. Several boats had rudder and rig failures. This is scary stuff. I am afraid that the envelope has been pushed a bit too far. I am hoping that there will be a stepping back from the edge with a careful evaluation of what went wrong. I also hope that the process of studying the problem ... will not see some knee-jerk reaction that will force a halt to the development of boats for these most challenging venues.

I agree with Jeff that the testing and development of these extreme racers performs a useful goal. I also see the negative aspects of the Vendee Globe race as a wake-up call to keep these developments at arm's length from the typical cruising boat. I wrote back to Jeff:

> I admire Ian McCurdy tremendously. The lack of extremes in his work is a sign of strength; he doesn't need gimmicks to produce great boats. Moderation in cruising designs is something I've been trying to get across to you for years. C.A. Marchaj has similar things to say in his second book, *Seaworthiness, the Forgotten Factor*.
>
> A distinction must be made between a boat that *can* sail well and one that *must be* sailed well. Offshore cruising conditions demand a boat that is forgiving and that will take care of its crew. A boat that is punishing *and* needs constant attention to survive may win a race with a large and athletic crew, but it will endanger a smaller, weaker one.
>
> In coastal conditions, a high rate of speed may allow you to outrun weather and spend the worst of it at anchor. At sea, while the ability to maneuver around storms is of some benefit (getting into a more favorable quadrant, limiting the exposure time to the chance of bad weather developing, etc.), long periods (24 to 72 hours) of horrible conditions may have to be endured. During much or all of that time, an exhausted or injured crew may not be able to sail the boat and must rely for support on the seakeeping qualities of the craft.
>
> I think McCurdy's point on water ballast is also well taken. The Whitbread boats are not, in my opinion, a useful comparison. They are for driven athletes in intense competition, and they adopt any expedient that will give them an edge.
>
> This brings me to a problem we're running into with Navy Point: the conflicts of light displacement with the need for a cruising payload and a high ballast ratio. At a realistic cruising weight of 16,000

pounds, the last version had a too-low ballast ratio, especially if no allowance was made for water ballast. In your last request, you wanted to increase the ballast *and* narrow up the waterline aft....

I think we need a bottom-line weight estimate, including cruising gear and stores, a range of acceptable ballast ratio, so I can give you a hull that will support them with a prismatic coefficient that is reasonable. In the meantime, we are at cross-purposes and playing tug-of-war.

A fast cruiser will not be as fast as a racer of comparable size. It can be close.

The latest sail plan for Navy Point incorporates a more conventionally proportioned sail plan and the longer cabin/shorter cockpit we've talked about. I was hoping you would send me the layout sketch you promised.... I'll wait for that before making any changes to the accommodation plan.

On my recent trip to Maine to look at a Morgan Giles sloop I

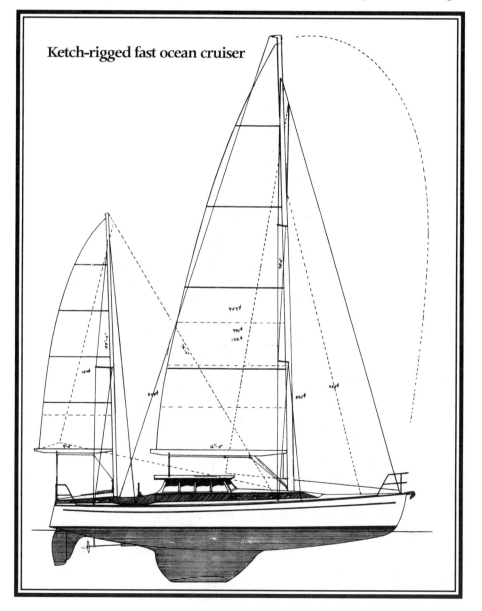

Ketch-rigged fast ocean cruiser

Cartoon for a more moderate off-shore Navy Point

87

hope to buy as my "floating test bed," I had another look at Marchaj's book on seaworthiness. The combination of my experience on the moderately heavy Giles boat (9,700 pounds on LOA 30 feet and LWL 25 feet), and my reading, continue to reinforce my feeling that the ideal offshore cruising boat should have more displacement and more wetted surface than you would care to see.

I look forward to working on a series of boats with moderate beam, more balanced ends, higher displacement, and more lateral plane (the ketch-rigged fast ocean cruiser for example.) In the meantime, let's see if the current Navy Point isn't close enough to what you are after to hold us until the project is ready to get underway. At that stage, we can take this groundwork and hammer out whatever changes the intervening time brings forth.

Subsequent discussions have brought out Jeff's focus on sailing on the Chesapeake Bay. Many of the points I've argued against are problems for more open waters and don't apply to Chesapeake sailing. There are no opportunities for heaving-to on the Chesapeake, for example, nor are there swells of any size. All trips are of necessity short, with anchorages always within range. Questions of endurance don't have the same import as they do in more exposed locations. Early on in this project, I was thrown off by Jeff's mention of future extensive cruising. As specific issues have arisen during the design process, his focus has become clearer to me.

The continued problems we've had with this design are illustrative of the kinds of things that can go wrong with a commission. For that reason alone, this chapter is valuable if we are to explore more fully the possibilities of custom design.

There are still many loose ends in our interaction. Jeff and I continue to debate points, and the design moves on to different configurations. The reasons for this are many and not easy to pin down. In part, the hypothetical nature of the project has kept us from having to focus on a particular goal. Each is free to speculate and keep speculating. Of all the commissions in this book, Navy Point has the tightest reins held by the client. Jeff, as an architect with his own ambitions in yacht design, has kept very close to his own vision of what the boat should be. I've taken the commission as an opportunity to explore my own interests, even when they're opposed to Jeff's views.

Most cases of successful boat-design collaboration come to an equilibrium between the client's wishes and the designer's ideas. None of the difficulties in this project to date are insurmountable. Jeff and I look forward to continuing our debates, and to creating designs together out of the fruits of these interactions. Jeff's high level of experience and knowledge of the subject keep our debates interesting and productive.

The true gridlock arises when a client with a lot of authority in his or her own field is unwilling to relinquish authority to a designer. In such a case, the outcome is rarely successful. A designer cannot wrest authority from a client; it must be given. It's crucial to realize that the true exercise of power often resides in delegating responsibility, as well as being open to the happy surprises that may result.

Beyond the tension between our viewpoints, the inherent difficulties of designing a boat with racing pretensions have compounded our problems. Racing adds so much complexity to a design, lengthening the spiral beyond the evolutions needed for a cruising boat or daysailer. For our purposes here, we'll have to leave Navy Point as a work in progress. Our debate, we hope, will be continued in other fora.

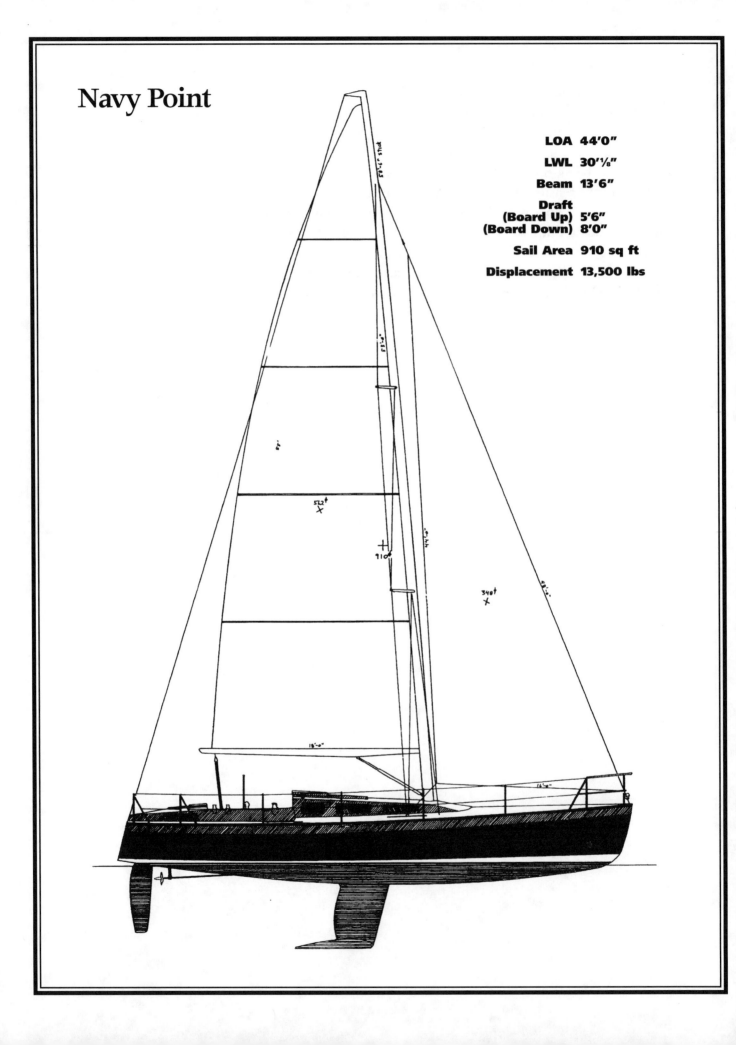

Navy Point

LOA	44'0"
LWL	30'⅛"
Beam	13'6"
Draft (Board Up)	5'6"
(Board Down)	8'0"
Sail Area	910 sq ft
Displacement	13,500 lbs

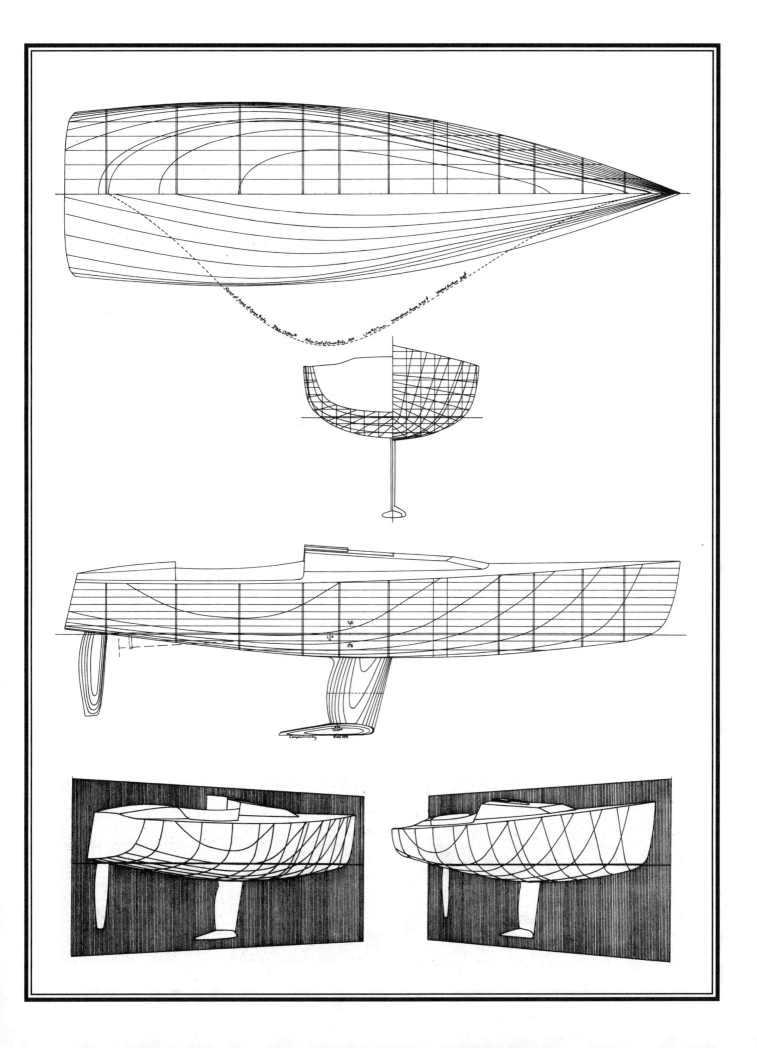

Navy Point

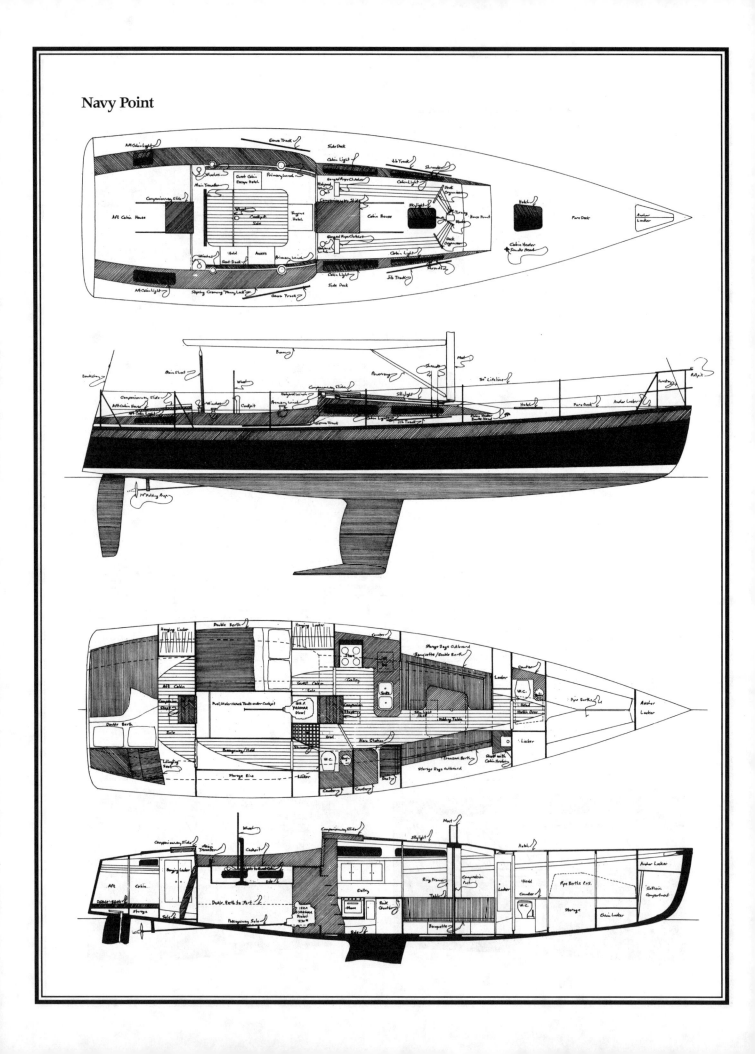

CHAPTER 5

Castle Hill

Peter H. Spectre is well known as a journalist, author, and editor in the marine field. His role in this book is twofold. As the editor, he has helped shape its form and content; as one of the featured clients, his interest has taken some curious turns. When we started this project, Peter and his wife, Eileen, had recently bought a 27-foot Atkin powerboat. They were looking for a modest tender.

Peter, however, was interested in a tender with a difference. My notes from our phone conversation describe a boat based on the utilitarian yard punt, a garvey type used to work around boats at the mooring. He wanted it to be a good flatwater rowing boat for pottering about in the harbor as well.

The first requirement for such a craft is extreme stability; the boat must be able to handle an adult standing amidships while painting a rail or overhauling a bobstay. The boat should row well with one oarsman and perhaps a passenger. Freeboard will be low, but there will be a stout rail, well guarded. The hull form is that of a garvey, with a curved entry and run and a flat bottom with no flare amidships. The added attraction? Extreme simplicity of construction.

Such a boat will live banging against a float, or "drug up the fore-shore," so construction needs to be rugged. The boat will be rowed in flat water; expecting rough-water capability would be asking too much of this hull form. A certain amount of weight should not adversely affect its intended performance. Besides helping with longevity and making it less skittish as a work platform, the added inertia may help to overcome the relative bluntness of the entry.

A sprinter needs to be light to accelerate rapidly. Pottering about requires a different rhythm. A few solid strokes will start the boat moving, but then you might look around, absentmindedly trailing the oars. When an infernal machine suddenly roars by, leaving clouds of blue smoke and a curling wake, a light punt would stop dead (at best) on hitting a wave. This boat will absorb the shock and keep moving.

This heavy, stolid, reliable workhorse can become a helper that fades into the task to be performed with no need for special treatment or further thought. At play, it demands a certain deference due his worker's physique—handsome, but lacking adornment.

The first conversation was followed up by a letter from Peter a few weeks later, when he elaborated on the premise:

> If you could have seen me trying to paint the caprail on my boat from the water last summer, you would know exactly why I am look-ing for the design of a yard boat. My mooring was in Rockland, Maine, near the ferry landing, and I was working from a rowing skiff that was handsome and fast but on the tender side. It seemed as if every time I reached a critical point on the job— cutting in at the stem, for example—the Vinalhaven or North Haven ferry would go by, throwing up a big wake. My skiff would rock, it would roll, paint would go flying, and I'd grab for the nearest secure handhold. It would always be the part of the caprail I had already painted....

The yard skiff at a nearby boatyard caught Peter's eye. But why "design" such a basic boat at all? Peter had an answer for that:

> It may seem odd to ask a professional for the design of a yard skiff, a harbor craft for working on other, larger vessels. Most are probably designed by the builder as he goes along. The criteria are obvious and not particularly difficult to achieve: strength, durability, stability. No need to make the boat light; no need to worry about looks....
>
> I'm looking for a professional design because this boat will be used privately, not in a shipyard. I will be working in it during spring fitting-out and periodic summer maintenance, and not much more. The rest of the time, I'd like to have it for general use around the har-bor. It could be used for pleasure rowing, and as a ferry for bringing visitors and provisions out to my boat from the shore, something with a tad more capacity than the usual tender.... It could also be used as a winter boat, the one left in the water all year. If it were

strong enough, it could take the ice; if it were easy enough to row, it would be perfect for a quick trip out to the island on those relatively good days that fall between the nasty ones deep in the heart of December, January, and February.

Peter listed his priorities in stream-of-consciousness fashion:

Stout, strong, durable, not complex in construction, 8 to10 feet long, built from locally obtainable materials, heavy knees, very stable (I should be able to stand in it while working alongside), primarily for rowing but able to take a self-contained outboard, 2 hp or so, skids on the bottom so it can be pulled up on the rocks, padded rubrails, with a certain amount of shape so it doesn't look like a box, not slabsided so it will gain buoyancy as it is loaded and so only the rubrail makes contact with whatever it lies alongside, no plywood except maybe in the bottom.

In my mind's eye, I see this boat with two lapped side planks, cross-planked bottom, blunt at the ends, two-tone gray (dark and light), handsome but not pretty—the ambiance of Oshkosh overalls fresh from the wash. In style, it would have elements of Pete Culler, Billy Atkin, and the punt Walt Kelly's cartoon character Pogo used to row around the Okefenokee Swamp with his friends....

You might look up Pete Culler's sampan, which is in his book *Skiffs & Schooners*, and a couple of his punt doodles on page 14 of his book *Boats, Oars, and Rowing*. And also look at page 8, an Atkin punt built by Rich Kolin; it's a bit on the light side, but wide for its length.

I had begun work based on the earlier phone call, before I received the letter. My first impressions had led to a V-bottomed pram 18 feet long, which took the "yard skiff" idea a bit further than Peter had really wanted. The first hull, worked up in Maxsurf, was meant to be long enough to row well and not to need too much beam for stability.

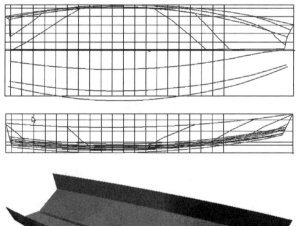

It's often forgotten that length has a greater effect on stability than beam. Of course, if the length is constant, the wider hull is more stable, but a hull gains stability more readily by growing longer than by growing wider. Any increase in size will add to resis-

18′ yard skiff screen shots

tance, since this is a function of wetted surface at low speeds. Added length lowers the wavemaking resistance and raises the boat's hull speed. For a rowing boat, this means that the longer boat is easier to push, and it can have a higher practical speed than a wide, short boat.

What the first skiff traded for these gains was compactness and economy of construction. The second draft was for a 10-foot sampan skiff. The calculations showed this to have enough capacity for the intended uses. As a flat-bottomed boat, considerably shorter in length, it had the pluses of lower materials costs and improved ease of construction.

One of the benefits of using the surface modeling program Maxsurf on a simple design like this is evident from the printouts of the boat in a wave train, and with the crew weight off-center. In the pre-computer days, a simple skiff would warrant only the most sketchy of hydrostatic calculations; they're just too time-consuming when done manually. Now it only takes moments to obtain numerical and pictorial representations of the results.

My next communication with Peter brought a radical change of tack. When he called to talk over some general editorial matters, the conversation turned to musings of a much more intriguing nature. He and Eileen had been thinking about the possibility of building a larger boat than their 27-foot Atkin. He broached the subject of another powerboat, one large enough to spend considerable time aboard and serve as a floating writer's office (or, one could also say, a writer's floating office). A boat to cruise the Intracoastal Waterway. The 27-footer was too small for this mission. The proposed new boat should stay simple, with few systems. It would be large enough for two people to get away from each other as needed, if protracted periods are spent aboard.

Not long after that phone conversation, a follow-up letter arrived:

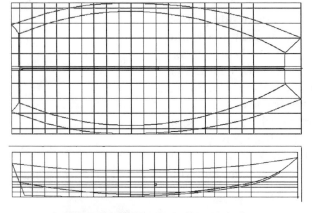

10' sampan skiff screen shots

I've always had an interest in powerboats, though I never did much about it. Had a semi-dory with an outboard once, and a small Banks dory with an outboard well. (If you ever feel tempted by a well, take a cold shower and forget about it.) But I never had an inboard-powered anything before last year.

After our last child graduated from college, we discovered that more money was sticking to us than theretofore. (At one point, we had three children in college at the same time....) Eileen pointed out that she was ready to go cruising along the Maine coast in what she called a "real" boat, not a rowboat. Frankly, I wasn't sold on the idea. I've always been a small-boat man. My favorite boat, the one I will never sell, is a 27-pound decked-over Wee Lassie type, the 10½-footer built by Bart Hauthaway, the model he calls the Rob Roy.

Peter came to the conclusion that he didn't really want a sailboat. After chartering a pocket cruiser, a sailboat, and enjoying the cruise, he turned down a chance to buy it:

"Why?" Eileen wanted to know. I couldn't say. We had the money, we had the time.... Why not?

The truth was that when it came to boats I consider to be large—i.e., anything in which you can set up housekeeping—I had something else in my mind's eye. So I started describing it to her. I talked and talked and talked and talked. Eileen listened, then nodded her head and picked up the latest edition of *Soundings* and flipped to the classified-ad section.

"You mean like this boat?" she asked, pointing to a photograph. I put on my reading glasses. "Yup," I said, "that's the one."

"That's the one" was listed as a 27-foot pilothouse cruiser designed by John Atkin, and it ripped my heart out. It had an enclosed wheelhouse with a visored straight-up-and-down windshield, a trunk cabin, lots of freeboard, and a sheer so pure it could make you weep. There were berths for two, with a spare in the wheelhouse, an enclosed head, and a simple galley. It was, of course, a powerboat. The power was a 36-hp diesel, not much bigger than your average auxiliary sailboat engine.

We were looking for a destination boat—a boat that got you where you wanted to go. A summer cottage afloat. Getting there wouldn't be the fun; being there would be. When we tired of the view, we could move her to another harbor or cove. You can do that on a sailboat, of course, but a powerboat provides more room, length for length, for the summer-cottage part.

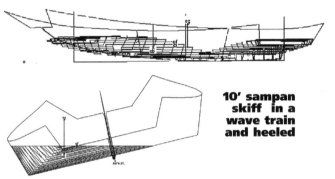

10' sampan skiff in a wave train and heeled

And that's how Peter and Eileen got *Monomoy*, the Atkin 27-footer that proved very satisfactory for cruising the coast of Maine. "She's a fine summer cottage," Peter reported, "but not really adequate as a home-away-from-home for a couple who are— how shall we say?—pushing the outer envelope of middle age."

He added that he was after some different qualities in the next boat. She needs to be in the 30- to 34-foot range and have a low-powered, full-displacement hull. While this leads naturally to a narrow hull, Peter is concerned about rolling. She will have a similar overall look to the Atkin design, with a wheelhouse and plenty of light and air.

He wants to take advantage of an often-overlooked perk of a new boat—she should have adequate headroom. It's my contention there is a middle ground between the traditional boat with stooped headroom and a contemporary design with slab sides and full headroom. I try to combine a lower profile, at least apparently so, and full headroom. Since our eyes have become more accustomed to higher freeboard than was typical years ago, a boat can have sufficient height for us to stand up straight and still seem sleek compared to contemporary designs.

Peter requested accommodations "for two friendly people (in

Designer & Client   other words, a double bunk or V-berths are fine), plus settees in the wheelhouse that can be converted to two guest berths." Engine access is important on a powerboat; it can't be an afterthought. The engine needs to be easily accessible for maintenance and, when the time comes, removable for a major overhaul.

A chart table, an enclosed head, and plenty of storage space for long-term occupation must be included. Fancy systems, such as hot water and air conditioning, are not required, although it can be designed so a second owner can retrofit later. The galley will be simple

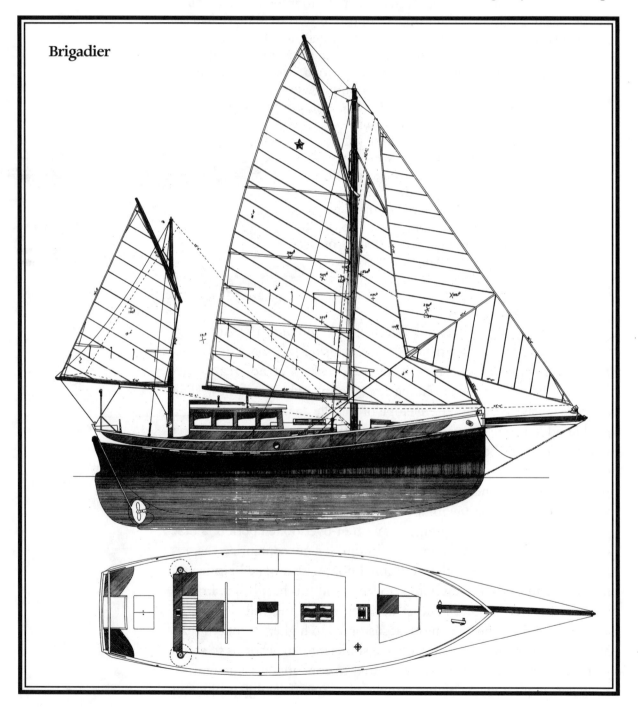

Brigadier

and workable, with propane stove, an icebox, electric and kerosene lighting, and a heating stove, either wood or kerosene. No generator, but provision for solar panels. In his letter, Peter added:

> I'll be paying our way south in my usual manner, as a writer, so I'll be needing a corner with a small table top (it could be fold-down, but preferably not) that will take a notebook computer and a pad of paper. Nearby, a cabinet for paper, pencils, reference books, etc., would be welcome.

Peter requested a dinghy either in davits or stowed on deck, plus "a riding sail to dampen rolling; the boom could be used to handle the dinghy if deck stowing is chosen.... This may be pushing things too far, but is it possible to have a minimal rig that will assist the engine and get us out of a jam if the engine quits altogether?"

I took that as an invitation to create a 70/30 motorsailer rig. While this would increase the building cost by about 25 percent, it would help control rolling and stretch the range a bit on passages off the wind.

Rounding out his list were honest anchors and provision for their use, a small electric winch, and a chain locker. Construction he left up to me. But he did have his opinion about aesthetics:

> The style I'm looking for is traditional-robust, if you know what I mean. Not a yacht (no varnish); a boat as defined by William and John Atkin, Carl Lane, and others of that ilk. Look at their motorboat designs; to my eye, they're the real things.
> To recapitulate: Simplicity with comfort. Handsomeness. Amenities for living aboard for months at a time. Economical operation. Working space for an itinerant scribbler.

At the time, I had a commission for the motorsailer *Brigadier*, and I felt that design would be a good starting point for Peter's boat. *Brigadier* is a heavy-displacement, full-powered auxiliary—pretty far over on the "sailer" side on the continuum of motorsailers. *Brigadier*'s owners had wanted a similar amount and quality of space in a boat of the same length, so I sent *Brigadier*'s accommodation plan to Peter.

Using a draft of *Brigadier* as a guide, I was able to work up a cartoon to give Peter at the Maine Boatbuilders' Show in March 1996. I find that these shows are good places to get together with clients. There isn't the uninterrupted time that would be available at a meeting in my office, but all the excitement of the show and the proximity to so many boats create a good atmosphere for talking over a design.

I like to have a boat name in mind when I work on a design, so if the client doesn't supply one soon enough, I tend to fill the gap. In Peter's case, I saw the boat as *Castle Hill*, after the hill of that name in Truro, on Cape Cod, where Peter lived for a couple of years when he was young. Coincidentally, I also grew up in Truro.

Designer & Client   Whenever I submit drawings to a client, I send two copies so that they can mark up a set with notes and return it with their comments. Peter's reaction to the outboard profile of the first draft of *Castle Hill* was positive—including the name—though he fell for the grand temptation to start "painting" the boat before the design was even completed. Of course, I recognize and share his desire. Here's what Peter proposed:

I'm thinking light gray topsides. Light-colored decks and housetops (the Sunny South, you see—this is a boat for the Ditch). House sides? Moldings? I don't know. Maybe off-white house; the moldings could be where we hit them with serious color. You're an artist. What do you suggest?

But I'm getting way ahead of myself. Have to get the boat itself right before we get into decoration.

My main concerns are that there should be standing headroom for me (6 feet 1½ inches, minimum) in the wheelhouse, under the end of the main boom, and under the mizzen boom; and that visibility fore and aft be unimpeded when I am at the wheel.

First draft with Peter's comments

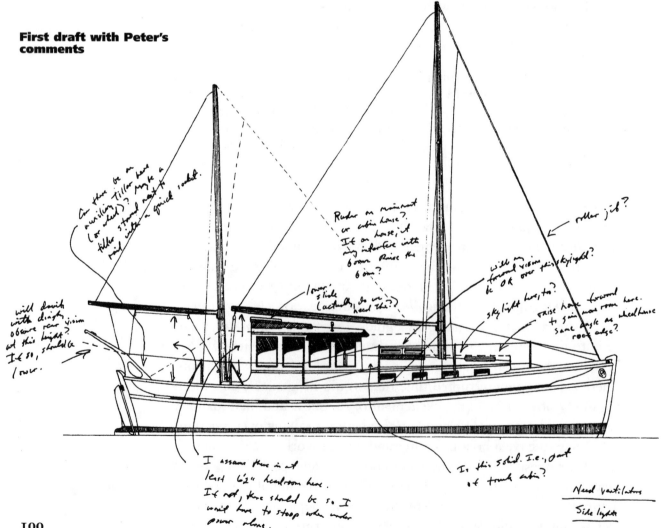

Another matter is the masts. Is there a way to rig them so they can be de-rigged without a great deal of effort to get under low bridges—in other words, without the services of a boatyard?

By the way, if the mast is going to be taken down at any time when the boat is still being used, the radar shouldn't go on the main-mast; better put it in the wheelhouse. In that case, the boom will have to be higher to clear the radar dome. But that could be a good thing, because it might simplify the rigging of awnings in the heat of the South.

The more I think about this boat, the more I like it.

I wrote to address the points Peter had raised:

I like your ideas on colors. I've always been partial to light green-ish gray, similar to the motorsailer *Burma*, but maybe a bit lighter, combined with off-whites and neutral grays on trim and moldings. On the other hand, as you say, the trim—or at least the cove at the scupper line and the boottop—are the spots to put strong color. The choice of colors will strongly affect the character of the vessel. Pastels may have a place, providing a Bermudan feeling: a sharp yellow cove with a cobalt boottop, or a vibrant red cove with an emerald green boottop.

At this point I began developing a new format to present draw-ings. Blueprints are luscious, but it is hard to coordinate, or even jus-tify, trips to the blueprinter when I can scan and then print out my drawings in my office as needed. Since the hull lines exist in virtual full scale in a Maxsurf computer file, there is no need to draw these early drafts at large scales on paper. It's easier to visually grasp a smaller drawing, while dealing with details in exploded views. Lower mailing charges and "e-mailability" play a part here, also.

Before continuing, then, let's digress for a moment to the subject of computer-aided design (CAD). I have yet to come to a "system" for dealing with the complications of combining traditional hand draw-ings with CAD. Each has its place and each has its faults; I have tried to coordinate the two. Nothing beats the fluidity of hand drawing for correcting details of proportion and for presenting the boat in a "liv-ing" way. On the other hand, the ease of accurate measurement and analysis of hull forms that Maxsurf allows cannot be achieved on paper. Likewise, the organization and accuracy of working in Mini-cad adds another kind of fluidity to the process. For example, it is possible to just "grab" whole sections of a drawing and shift them around.

There isn't an easy or obvious way to integrate these methods, however. I know of some design firms, frustrated by the limitations, that have abandoned CAD and returned exclusively to hand drawing. I'm not ready to do that, and I don't have the staff to replace the speed and accuracy of the Power Mac. Still, I bring a traditionalist's skepticism to the whole matter. I'm not willing to throw out the old for the new, yet not quite willing to do the opposite, either!

And now back to Peter's project, and my letter accompanying the second draft:

The outboard profile should address the points you brought up in the last round. Visibility is improved. The headroom is there, rest assured; it was there from the start! So is the ventilation. I've exchanged the companionway (it was there as a way to open up the wheelhouse in good weather and not for head clearance) for a windscreen for the wheel in the cockpit. The steering lines run to a tiller under a grate at the stern. An extension will allow for emergency steering.

I've put the radar on the mizzen. This raises it a bit without putting it so high that it creates excessive windage and is adversely affected by rolling or heeling. The mizzen staysail sheets to the mizzen boom, at the sailmaker Nat Wilson's suggestion. In his opinion, the staysail alone should make the rig worthwhile. I also think the higher transverse moment of inertia caused by the rig will help soften the motion even without raising sail.

Minor modifications

The moment of inertia is a measure of the way a boat either gains or loses motion due to inertia. As a boat responds to wave action with either a roll or a pitching motion, the higher moment of inertia, caused by significant weights far from the gravitational center, slows and dampens the motion. Too much damping can put a boat out of synch with the sea and make the boat excessively wet. The more frequent case is a boat with too little damping that snap-rolls and pitches violently. There is no substitute for some ballast and mast height on a powerboat to raise the moment of inertia and quiet these motions.

My letter to Peter continued:

The masts are on tabernacles so they will cradle each other when lowered. The main rests in a crutch off the mizzen tabernacle, and vice versa. An anchor davit will assist the winch in handling the ground tackle.

I think the hull is shaping up. I've kept the prismatic coefficient fairly low (.56), in line with your desire for a low-powered, economical cruiser.

The prismatic coefficient (or prismatic) is a measure of the proportion of a "prism" encompassing the underbody of the hull that is taken up by the actual underbody of the boat. Imagine that you were to take the hull and slice it off at the waterline. Then turn it over and cover it with a gabled roof. The percentage of the volume under the roof taken up by the hull is the prismatic coefficient.

Some sailboats have a prismatic as low as 49 percent—i.e., the actual hull takes up 49 percent of the total prismatic shape. The prismatic coefficient can be closely linked to the optimum speed/length ratio for a hull. Generally, the lower the prismatic, the less resistance at low speed/length ratios. The low speed resistance rises as the coefficient is made fuller, but the maximum potential speed/length ratio is increased with it. For sailboats, whose power is limited by the ability to carry sail and the vagaries of wind speed, the optimum prismatic coefficient is relatively low, typically ranging from 50 percent to 55 percent. In powerboats, the optimum coefficient is tied to the desired speed/length ratio and to the powerplant available. The range here is much broader—from 55 percent for low-speed, low-power hulls to 80 percent for tugs, or destroyers having very high power for their size.

More comments from me for Peter:

The displacement is 12,600 pounds. There can be 3,000 pounds of ballast and 3,750 pounds of fuel, along with generous stores. The ballast will help with the motion as well as stability under sail. The fuel will give a generous, even intercontinental range.

I've hung the Gentleman's Yard Punt [the name I came up with for Peter's yard punt] from the davits. It was irresistible, although I think the punt is a bit low-sided to be an all-purpose dinghy. Perhaps it would be best to have a shortened version of Jenny Bennett's sailing dinghy [see first chapter], serving as an all-weather tender suitable for running out a kedge in bad weather as well as for pottering about an anchorage. Leave the punt at your spring-maintenance port.

I then went on to finalize the exterior and concentrate on the interior. Here are Peter's comments on the results:

What can I say? It's a piece of work. When I was a boy and the thought of running away from my responsibilities racketed through my head—and that thought came around at least once a day—this is the type of craft I dreamt of doing it in. Not too big, not too small, the principal amenities but nothing too complex or difficult to maintain, a few sails and lines to fool around with but motor power to get her where I wanted her to go, when I wanted to go there. Thanks for all that.

I know that as the commissioner of a custom design I'm supposed to run down a long list of demands, criticisms, and complaints, but I've never been that type. I think you have to grow up broke to appreciate that just having a boat is good enough, that trying to make the boat perfect is being greedy or something. (The carpenter who is working on my house right now finds my attitude a trifle baffling. I tell him I want a cabinet over the kitchen counter. He asks me what it should look like. I tell him to use his own best judgment. He builds the cabinet and, with fear and trembling in his voice, asks me what I think. I tell him that it looks great to me. I'm just grateful I can afford to have a cabinet built.)

Anyway, to prove that I have been paying attention, I have a few comments that are just that—comments. There is no need to integrate them into the design, because (a) they're just about niggling, inconsequential matters, or (b) they can be worked out in the construction of the boat or underway when we're putt-putting down the Intracoastal Waterway.

I know why you have such a slope to the forward end of the trunk house—to provide visibility for the helmsman—but if I were rowing around my boat and looking at her profile, I'd want the roofline of the trunk house to be more or less parallel to that of the wheelhouse. I'd even suffer having to crane my neck to look over the bow in order to achieve such a lovely profile.

Right now, I have an anchor lashed down on the foredeck of my Atkin motorboat. It's a colossal pain; it seems as if I'm always tripping over the damned thing, plus all sorts of debris gets trapped under it. Better to have it lashed to the rail, or on top of the trunk cabin, or—where? No wonder those stemhead anchor chocks have become so popular.

I know two are supposed to be better than one, but as the gent who doesn't cook and therefore always gets to wash the dishes, I'd rather have a single large sink than two small ones.

See what I mean? Not much in the comments and complaints department.

You know and I know that the glitches in this design, if there are any, won't show up at this stage in the plans anyway. They'll appear during construction, or when we're motoring through the Cape Cod Canal, or when I'm trying to meet a writing deadline and Eileen is trying to cook a meal at the same time.

I do have a question, though. How much is it going to cost to build this boat? Actually, I'm a little late in asking that. It seems to me that the smart way to proceed on something like this is to start with an amount and try to achieve a boat that can be built for that amount. The arrogant way is J.P. Morgan's ("If you have to ask...."). The stupid way is to ask now. The really, really dumb way is never to ask, to have her built and see what the bill comes to when launched.

Peter was right, the items he might want to change are best left for the construction phase. I always recommend mocking up the interior so that minor corrections, or major modifications, can be made when they can be readily grasped and before anything irrevocable has been done. These "fittings" are an important part of making the boat the owners'. Counter heights, bunk widths, etc., can be adjusted to actual preferences. It will be an easy matter to mock up the sight lines from the wheelhouse to see just how much head craning Peter would be willing to put up with for the sake of that parallel coach roofline.

I wrote back to Peter with my thoughts about that vital matter, money:

In my estimation, *Castle Hill* can be built for something between $170,000 and $210,000. This is based on a range of $12 to $15 per pound. This is a feasible rate from a small builder with low overhead, the kind of place Billy Atkin always preferred. You'll need to obtain a more detailed estimate from a short list of builders. A large part of the cost of a boat is tied to the systems and level of finish desired. A boat like this one, as you've requested, can do without the more elaborate systems and will look good with a "workboat" finish, so these costs can be kept down.

Doing some or all of the finishing work yourself, and taking care of the detailing, can bring considerable savings. I recommend this as a better option than trying to build the hull and major structures yourself—especially for someone with limited boatbuilding experience. That way, the major structures are built accurately and efficiently. The owner's contribution then is an additive process, working on bits and pieces that can be handled easily. Mistakes are easier to deal with. In the worst case, if tasks seem too daunting, the professional can take the boat farther toward completion. If an amateur has messed up the hull, it is a little late to try to bring in pro-

Final profile and deck plan with some thoughts on anchors and anchoring

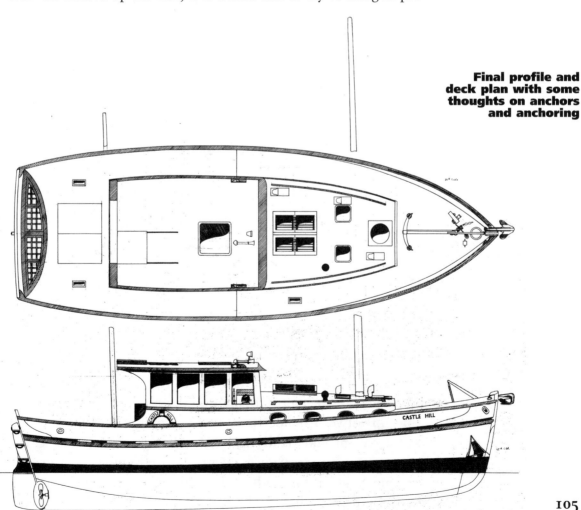

fessional help. At the least, expensive remedial work will be in order.

A method for lowering the cost that is too-seldom used would be to find buyers for multiples of the boat. If two or three of you approach a builder together, there will be substantial savings. You will be able to amortize the setup costs over the run of vessels. Materials and equipment can be purchased at better rates as well. Even more ambitiously, find a builder interested in producing fiberglass hulls and offer your hull as his prototype. These options require more entrepreneurial skills than boatbuilding ones. For that reason, they can be useful options for people who have more business experience under their belts than time on the end of a jack plane.

Boats cost by the pound, so it's difficult at the design stage to come up with an exact figure. There are just too many variables. The best that can be done is to predict a certain range of cost, and to get bids from builders. The cost range I gave Peter for *Castle Hill* is based on the assumption that the boat would be built in a small Maine yard with low overhead. With its "workboat" finish, the boat wouldn't have any "yachty" systems to crank up the cost.

The most common way to work out the building of a custom design is first to complete the drawings and then submit the plans to a number of builders for bids. Then the owner and the designer can meet (if possible) with the builders and get a sense of their capabilities and the reasonableness of their figures. Then the owner awards the contract to the chosen builder.

Another option is to start the entire process with a builder in mind. Needless to say, this works best when the builder is someone the designer or owner has worked with previously. The builder is included in the whole design phase. His input can help streamline the construction schedule so it best fits his common practice while still meeting the designer's standards and the owner's needs. With such an arrangement, and if time is an important factor, construction can even begin before the design is finalized, with drawings prepared before they're needed.

When someone buys a stock plan, or even when there is a basic contract for a custom design, the mechanics of getting a builder and dealing with construction are left up to the client. It's possible, however, for an owner to contract with the designer to act as an agent in finding and supervising a builder.

Your choice of builder will be dictated by circumstance and your preferences. In keeping with my overall philosophy, I feel that the relationship between builder and owner should be a relatively personal one. I recommend small yards that are committed to fine work. A boat-construction project is no place to rely on an adversarial relationship built on low bids and penalty clauses. You just can't force people to produce the good results you expect.

Choose people you can trust and then become part of the team. Get involved as a participant, not an overseer. The work will go better, you'll know more about the boat, you'll be much more likely to enjoy the whole drama of construction, and you'll appreciate your boat even more after you launch her.

Castle Hill is waiting on the page for the chance to take form. Peter goes back and forth in his thinking about whether or not to follow through and have her built. Stay tuned.

Many boats never get past the dream stage, of course. There may still be an advantage in taking a dream through the preliminary design stage. The dream gains a certain life on paper. Even though time may pass before the project can be carried on to concrete reality, the drawings are like a flag—looked up to when the going gets tough. As time passes, they provide fodder for meditation, and the thinking behind them can be further refined. This groundwork may mean that the boat may yet be built at some point when circumstances are more propitious.

As with all the boat designs developed in this book, I can see a general utility to *Castle Hill* beyond Peter's own commission. There are many people today whose work doesn't hold them to a particular spot—not just writers and artists, but others in the "information" business who need no more than a desk, a computer, and a modem to produce their work.

A previous generation looked forward to retirement in the sun with a multidecked sportfisherman parked out on some canal. Times have changed, and that equation, for good or ill, is harder and harder to resolve. On the other hand, we can look forward to the kind of working retirement described by Peter—afloat on a modest cruiser, whether sail or power, with or without a "pied-a-terre" somewhere to act as a home base. Keep the costs low (at least compared to buying waterfront property), carry your "office" with you, and live the nomadic life.

Castle Hill

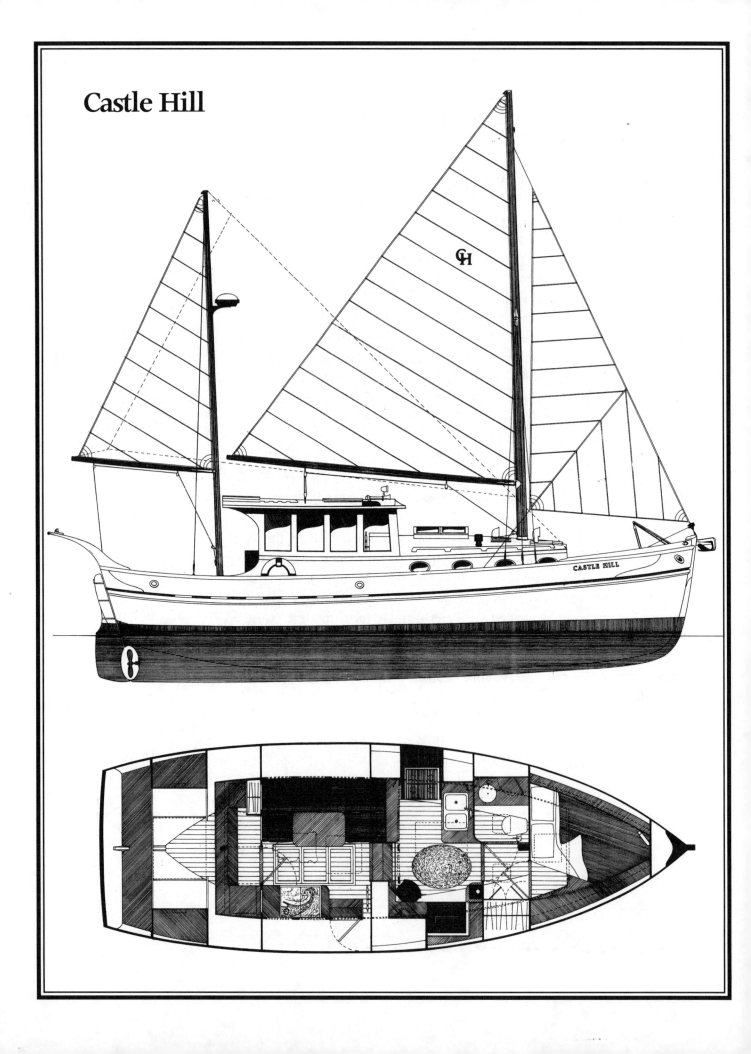

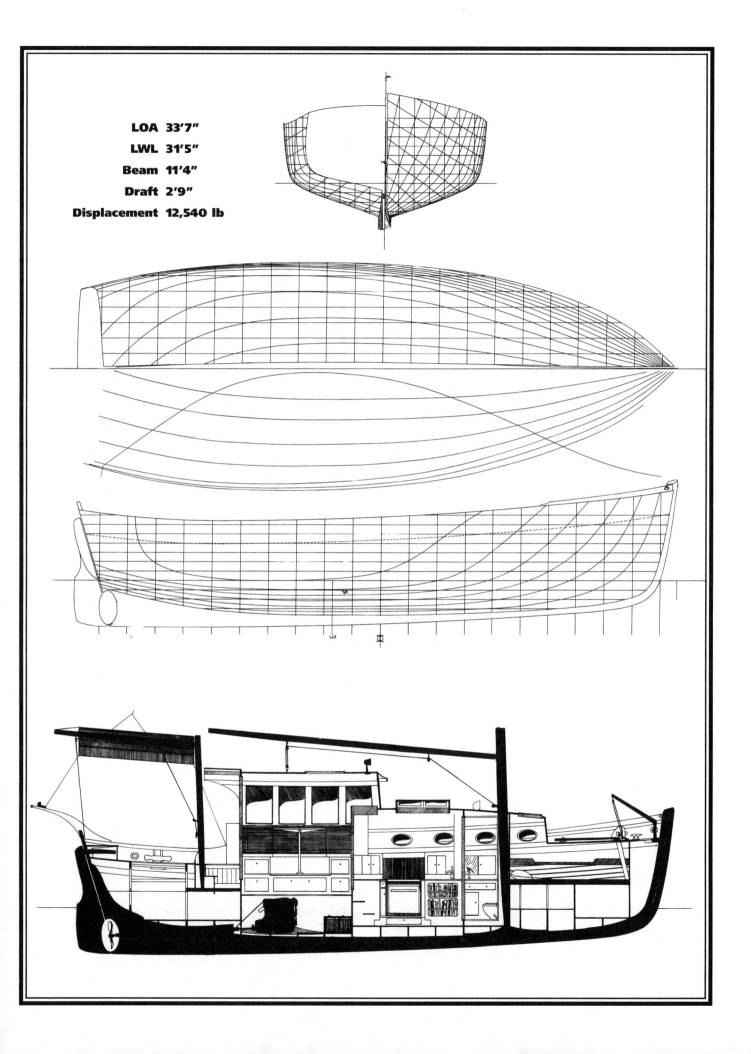

LOA 33'7"
LWL 31'5"
Beam 11'4"
Draft 2'9"
Displacement 12,540 lb

CHAPTER 6

17′ Cruising Kayak

Mike O'Brien is a man with a great deal of boating experience: senior editor at *WoodenBoat* magazine, editor and publisher of *Boat Design Quarterly*, designer/builder, and veteran kayaker. As the latter, he was interested in a new custom cruising kayak.

I began with a Maxsurf-generated first draft and sent it to Mike. We talked it over in person at the Maine Boatbuilders' Show, and later he wrote me with his thoughts:

> I'm happy that you chose to draw a 27-inch beam. My original thoughts were for a slightly shorter (say, 15 foot 6 inch) length and greater width—perhaps 29 inches. We might still elect to go that way if you think the savings and convenience are worthwhile. (I should also add that the shorter LOA would exempt the boat from some USCG equipment regulations that are difficult for kayakers to satisfy....) In any case, I like the idea of making drawings available for boats of different widths (say, 24 to 29 inches) built to the same basic plans.
>
> Before you have a chance to draw them, I'd like to make a case against including bulkheads and hatches. In the relatively thin and flexible hulls of kayaks, bulkheads can create stress risers and make the hull more prone to fracture when riding over boulders and

beaver dams. Bulkheads trap water in the ends of the hull, where it cannot be bailed out easily. (On two occasions, I've been paddling offshore in company with expensive production kayaks when they began taking on water in their forward compartments. One leaked through a bad hatch-cover gasket, the other through a defective painter lead. Had their owners been paddling alone, they would have been in serious trouble.) I prefer having water collect amidships, where I can get rid of it.

Advertising notwithstanding, I've never seen a kayak hatch cover that didn't leak eventually. There seems to be no evidence that the Inuit ever built bulkheads into their kayaks (though they might have included them in some of their undecked boats). Certainly, we should encourage the use of flotation bags always, and seasocks in hard conditions. (Bulkheads and hatches might be shown as options.)

I'm glad that you didn't specify a rudder. They're expensive and/or labor-intensive to build, prone to mechanical failure, and difficult to rig with solid footbraces. Beginning paddlers tend to become dependent on them—at the expense of learning proper technique. Again, there seems to be no evidence of the Inuit having installed rudders on their kayaks until after the Russian corruption.

Would you want to draw out the run just a little and make the angle between keel and sternpost somewhat more crisp to ensure directional stability? Of course, trim is important here. Will the seat be adjustable forward and aft? (Perhaps not worth the complication.) In any case, how will the boat trim with the cockpit built as shown? A little down by the stern would be helpful. In the end, I don't think it would be a terrible thing if we had to add a shallow, skiff-style skeg (but not one of those shark fins that seem to be popular these days).

I worry a little that the high forward end of the cockpit coaming might bark my knuckles on occasion—but that's difficult to tell without a full-size mock-up. In any case, tall coamings seem not to hold spray skirts any better than low ones—both types need large lips or rims (1 inch is not too wide) to allow purchase for the skirt's hem. The roughly triangular shape of the cockpit as drawn will provide good thigh bracing (if the deck height is right). We might show a larger (say, 36 inch long) cockpit as an option.

The only real concern I have about paddling this boat in rough water is the relatively flat portion of the deck forward. I've seen similar arrangements suffer from the effects of considerable downward hydrodynamic forces when running off in a big sea. The boat might find the surface more easily and quickly if the deck forward were given more crown or peak—perhaps with the stem height increased an inch or two (which, in itself, would help reduce weathercocking). How to accomplish this without spoiling the boat's good looks I leave to you.

Appreciative of his general approval as well as his specific suggestions for improvements, I wrote back:

Your point against bulkheads and hatches is well taken. It makes sense from the safety angle as well as structurally, historically, and

Designer & Client

aesthetically. With a light line outhaul at each stempost, gear can be stowed beyond reach, and then retrieved by hauling on an inhaul. Light gear in watertight bags will provide almost as much extra flotation as watertight compartments, but without the weight, expense, and risks.

I'd rather not use a rudder. This is a general-purpose kayak, with greater-than-average beam. That makes the kayak a bit more forgiving than a narrow speedster, but I don't see this as an excuse for "dumbing down" the sport. By not relying on a rudder, the kayaker can, as you've put it, save on the complication and learn proper technique.

The run and the sternpost do need adjustment. This type of correction has been necessary in almost all my early drafts drawn in Maxsurf. There is no substitute for facing a hand-drawn draft on the drawing board to work out details of proportion and fine-tune lines. This is why I go back and forth between the computer model and the drafting table. I'll crisp up the sternpost and draw out the run.

Your last point, regarding the crown of the deck way forward, is a good one, It's easy to forget that a kayak is a wave-piercing hull form, and that water's effect on the "top" is as important as on the "bottom."

First draft

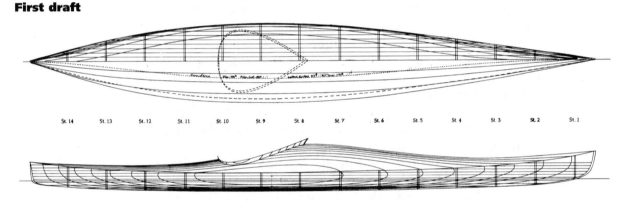

St. 14   St. 13   St. 12   St. 11   St. 10   St. 9   St. 8   St. 7   St. 6   St. 5   St. 4   St. 3   St. 2   St. 1

The debate about computer-assisted design (CAD) has long included the notion that a computer-designed boat must perforce look like a "modern" boat. It's thought that only simple, pared-down shapes are possible, or that the computer software can somehow "shape" (i.e., distort) the form against the designer's wishes. My years with Maxsurf have shown this not to be the case. Granted, it is easier to create simple, pared-down shapes on the computer, but that has always been true of hand drawing, too.

Maxsurf (I can't speak for the other programs, since I lack experience with them) has an interface that allows great flexibility in forming surfaces. There are procedures to learn, and experience grows with use—as with any medium worth its salt. A program won't design a hull for you. Maybe that's where some of the confusion has arisen. I liken working in Maxsurf to modeling in clay. The program gives you a clean lump, or a copy of a previously created form. It's up to the designer to make something of it—the same as ever.

One CAD limitation that I've mentioned a few times in these pages is that certain parts of the hull—a nice, flat run; the curve of a forefoot; a tapered rabbet line—can be difficult to achieve on the first try. Part of the problem lies with the difference between viewing a screen and looking at a sheet of drafting paper. Years of experience with paper and canvas have trained me to see and draw. Much of what happens is intuitive and occurs below the threshold of conscious volition. The old saw "if it looks right" is hard at work in comfortable surroundings. It takes time and effort to transfer those skills to the mouse and screen.

Another part of the problem lies in the method of shaping forms in a surfacing program. To put it very simply, the surface exists as a membrane stretched by various control points that act as "springs," tugging and pulling on it. You have control over their number, their placement, and the strength of their tugging. It's also possible to use one surface to "carve" away portions of another. This system has many strengths, the first of which is that it's adaptable to many possibilities of shape and form. It does take some doing to learn to adapt it to the specifics of creating a "traditional" hull form. For instance, I've had to "invent" my own method of creating a distinct rabbet line.

In the end, I find that the best way to deal with these problems is to go in and out of the computer environment. By using printouts as drafts for hand drawing, and then by scanning those drawings back into the computer to serve as templates for CAD forms, I can go back and forth between the two to find a middle ground between their respective qualities and shortcomings.

I incorporated Mike's suggestions in the second draft by developing the hull in Maxsurf, as a refinement of the earlier hull, and tracing them out by hand as a corrective to the loss of fine control over proportion and nuance that the small screen forced on me. I then sent the drawing to Mike with these comments:

> The bow is drawn out a bit, the deck peaked higher; the stern is more sharply curved at the foot. I've also added a small amount of rocker and fined the ends. The prismatic coefficient is therefore a bit lower at .525, easing the resistance at lower speeds without taking too much from the higher range. I noticed in the hydrostatic analysis that in a hull speed length wave, the middle of the hull was unsupported, the trough of the wave was below the keel. In actuality, a boat would never reach that point with a paddler's available power. I've attempted to compensate by fining the ends, adding rocker, and lowering the prismatic. This may be why kayaks never reach their theoretical hull speed.
>
> It's interesting that on such a long, fine hull, a lower prismatic may give a higher actual cruising speed. This is the opposite of what pinched ends will do to a shorter, deeper hull. The volume of the ends,

at deck level and above, has an effect on how the boat will behave, even in smooth water, due to the boat's wave train at high speed.

I don't think the height of the deck ahead of the coaming will interfere with paddling. The coaming at the front is 18 inches above the bottom, the deck ahead is 16 inches above the bottom. This will give room for the knees, and side support when maneuvering, but it shouldn't reach the knuckles.

No bulkheads are planned. The station markings are for the molds. Construction will be of ¼-inch cedar strips over NC-routed molds.

Perhaps I should explain this "NC" business. An NC router, or milling machine, is the "business end" of the CAD/CAM (computer-assisted design/computer-assisted manufacture) revolution. NC stands for "numerically controlled." The binary code of a CAD file is used to direct a robotic arm holding the cutting head: a router for wood or foam; a milling machine or cutting torch for metal. These machines range from portable units that can cut out molds for small boats to giant gantries that can mill out a plug for a mold for fiberglass boats up to 65 feet long.

Now back to my letter to Mike:

The hull will be planked in one stage, then the deck in a second stage. The hull/deck joint will be masked. After the deck is planked, the molds are removed and the deck and hull are joined. The inside of the hull's sheer will have a spruce stringer glued in place before the deck is attached. The deck will be epoxied and fastened to that stringer, then the outside of the joint will be taped with fiberglass and epoxy. The coaming will be laminated in spruce over a jig, and then glued into place on the deck. While the deck is off, the inside of the hull and deck will be fiberglassed and the outhaul tackle will be fitted into the boat's ends.

Although I know it's like paddling against a reversing falls to recommend this in most wooden kayak or canoe circles, I would like to see the boat painted. Parallel shiny strips of wood should be left for dance floors and bowling alleys. A boat, especially a shapely one, should show a unified surface. Otherwise, you can't see the shape for all the stripes. I'd rather see the boat in one of those fluorescent colors. (There's at least the added visibility.) I'd even rather see a broken pattern, two tones, or dazzle camouflage; they'd all show the shape better than strips, and they'd show a bit more originality in the bargain.

I'm not sure how you stand on this issue; I won't assume you're either with me or agin me, but I just had to speak out. It's good to have causes to champion, and the relative importance of them, in a cosmic sense, often has little to do with the satisfaction gained by espousing them.

You mentioned preferring to see a certain flexibility in the design to allow for different lengths and beams as well as different coaming sizes. To a certain extent, that can be obtained just by manipulating the molds, or the unfinished hull. This path, however, does open the door to the tinkerer to get into the usual trouble, with the result labeled a failure by the designer, not the tinkerer.

With CAD/CAM, I can provide a custom "cutter-path file" to the router for a boat to fit the owner without having to go through the physical process of lofting and fairing a set of molds. When done within the family of an existing design, it's relatively easy to dial in changes, fine-tune displacement to match the paddler's weight, and otherwise customize the boat. The router will cut to the new file just as readily. Standardization of the process instead of the product is the real revolution that CAD/CAM brings to design. I believe that in the future we'll be seeing this in everything from kayaks to automobiles.

Maxsurf printout with Mike's suggested changes

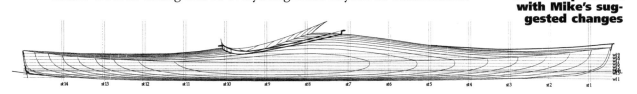

Not long afterward, Mike and I were able to find time to talk over the plans. It turns out I had misunderstood his comments about the rim of the coaming. We agreed that with the lower coaming, the deck itself should not cause trouble, while still providing legroom with knees bent. After our discussion, I made some revisions and sent them on to him; he sent back these comments:

> I think we're almost there—just a few items remain of concern.
>
> The cockpit is, almost certainly, too wide. The average width for contemporary sea-kayak cockpits seems to be about 17 inches. We will want to be able to wedge ourselves into the boat for better control when leaning and rolling. Although we can do this in a wide cockpit, it's not so easy or efficient. In addition, if we make the cockpit narrower, standard spray skirts will fit. As it's drawn, I believe we'll need a custom skirt.
>
> My comments about "height" in the last letter referred to the tall coaming, not to the height of the forward deck (which seems fine as is). While it is true that many Inuit boats show deep coamings, those coamings are close to the paddler (in some kayaks, up under his armpits). Strokes can be made with freedom and little danger of his hands striking the coaming. With the long cockpits that many of us now require, the coamings are nearly at arms' length. We're likely to bark our knuckles on the tall coamings as we sweep the paddle low across the deck for various maneuvering strokes and for rolling. Low coamings seem to hold spray skirts as well as do taller coamings. A wide (about 1 inch) coaming lip is essential.
>
> I'm glad you peaked up the sheer forward—better looking and better when running off in large waves, and it should help keep weathercocking in check. Are you concerned that the sharp upsweep forward will require short lengths of planking in that area? While this will cause only a slight inconvenience to the builder, the discontinuous appearance (if the boat is finished bright) might be disconcerting. Your point that these boats should be painted, so that our

Designer & Client

eyes can better follow the hull lines, is well taken. But builders need to understand the paradox that clear varnish hides imperfect fairing. Opaque, glossy paint exaggerates imperfections.

I'll continue to request a 36-inch-long cockpit option. It could be drawn as a dashed line on the same deck profile. Not every paddler will want the longer cockpit, but those extra few inches are important to some of us.

Have you crunched the numbers concerning location of the cockpit? Better to have it slightly too far aft than too far forward. Better yet to have it right on. Although I'm a believer in some preliminary hydrostatic calculations, I realize that the best way to ensure perfect balance would be to launch a prototype hull with a cockpit that is

Minicad screen shot

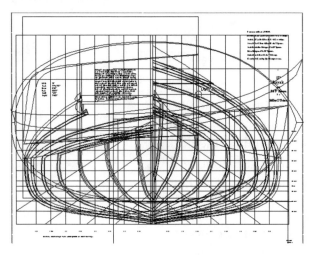

"adjustable" forward and aft. A flotation model might do if it were large enough to permit accurate scale measurements. In any case, the seat in the finished boat should be adjustable forward and aft through a range of at least 4 inches—to allow for sea conditions, trim adjustments according to the amount of stowed gear, and heading (forward for blasting to windward, farther aft for running off).

This will be a big and (relatively) stable kayak. The wetted-surface area seems to be about what most designers consider the maximum acceptable amount for a single kayak. But this boat has a sweet shape, and I believe it will be easy enough to propel at cruising speeds. In the hands of a strong paddler, it ought to have a higher top speed than many slinkier boats. The deck shape should help make rolling relatively easy, and the bottom shape should ensure that we don't often have to roll.

Our exchange ended there, with comfortable agreement—a relatively easy give-and-take, but of course a kayak design is much less involved than any of the other types we've examined in this book.

Before going on to another design, though, let's wrap up this matter of the role of CAD/CAM in boat design and boatbuilding.

The impact of CAD/CAM on shipbuilding has been to take the skilled work away from highly trained shipfitters and put it all in the CAD office. The CAD files are sent to a steel yard, where the plate is cut out with plasma cutters to the shapes shown on the drawings. All sorts of indexing marks, and even welding instructions, are marked on the plates. Notches and tabs are used to align parts almost in the way a plastic ship model goes together. This has reduced costs, but at the same time it has furthered the erosion of skilled labor that is a hallmark of our current industrial system. Nowadays, all you need is a field and a busload of neophyte welders and you've got a shipyard.

In amateur small-boat building, the same techniques can have a very different effect. Instead of simplifying work so that low-skilled labor can be exploited, CAD/CAM enables unskilled amateurs to accomplish more sophisticated construction than they could otherwise successfully complete.

In the past, all thinking relating to amateur construction centered on simplifying shapes so that beginners wouldn't be faced with lofting and precise fitting. As a result, the slab-sided boat built of sheet material became the epitome of amateur construction.

For decades, plywood made sense as a material for amateur boatbuilding. The simple shapes were easy to lay out, and the material was relatively inexpensive and fit into the experience of many "handy" types. I don't think the same holds true today. Marine plywood is very expensive, and quality has deteriorated over the last 10 years or so. As a result, many backyard builders now resort to inferior materials. This may be the only way for some to build a boat, but where alternatives do exist—and I'll get to those in a moment—it trivializes one's efforts to condemn a project from the start with risky and short-lived materials.

By combining strip/composite construction with the CAD/CAM techniques pioneered by shipbuilders, it's now possible for amateurs to build boats of any shape, and to do them at a cost comparable to that of a slab-sided plywood box. All of the boats shown in this book are examples in their own way, but I think Mike O'Brien's kayak is the purest case. A builder can start with a kit that has been customized to fit his or her size and weight. The forms can be cut to the exact dimensions with an NC router. A bundle of strips (milled to a bead-and-cove profile) and the necessary glue, epoxy, and cloth can all be included.

Perhaps the hardest thing for beginners to understand about round-bottomed boatbuilding is how the three-dimensional shape is captured in the building form. They may have some sense of what a lines plan is, and some idea of how it holds the key, but until they see with their own eyes how it all goes together, it remains a mystery. For many, it's a mystery that scares them away from trying to build boats with any shape. To these people, such a kit can be a revelation.

Once a beginner has put together a boat like this kayak—and seen how the process works after being guided by the designer and kit maker—the possibilities expand dramatically. The builder has not only the pride of having created a sculptural object but also the confidence to take on a more ambitious project. That next boat may be another full kit, or a set of plans with templates, or even a larger boat with offsets requiring lofting out the body plan. (With CAD-generated offsets, it isn't necessary to loft out the full lines.) Someone who previously felt capable only of building floating planter boxes has just started down the road to mastering one of the most satisfying skills there is.

17' Cruising Kayak

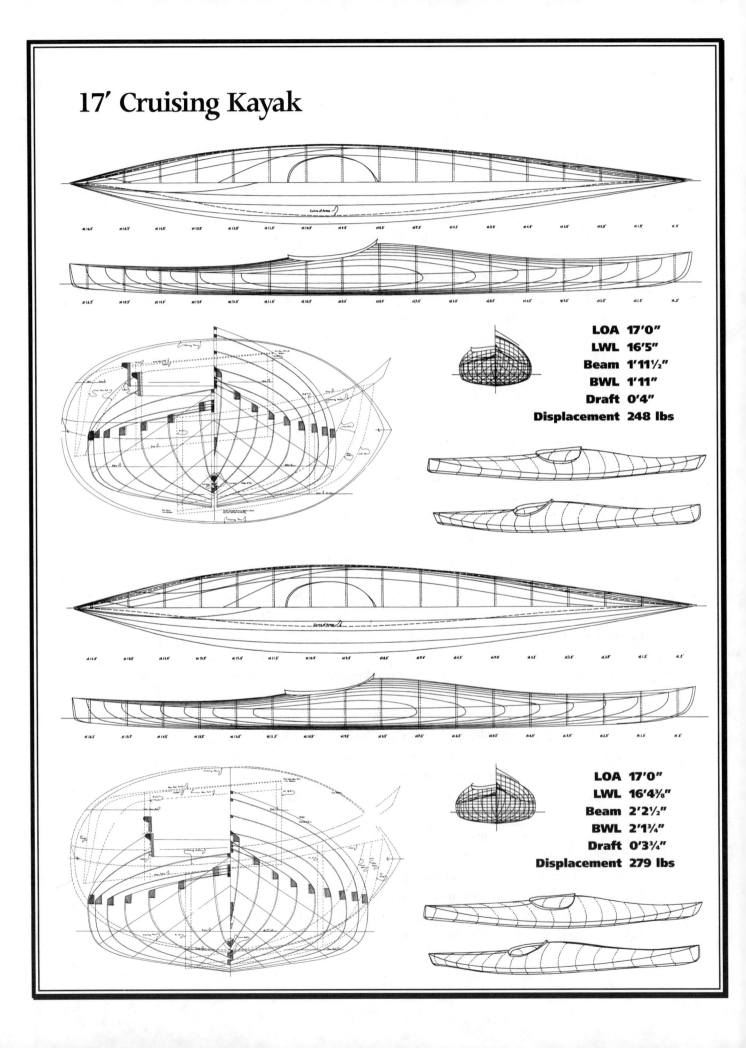

LOA 17'0"
LWL 16'5"
Beam 1'11½"
BWL 1'11"
Draft 0'4"
Displacement 248 lbs

LOA 17'0"
LWL 16'4⅜"
Beam 2'2½"
BWL 2'1¾"
Draft 0'3¾"
Displacement 279 lbs

CHAPTER 7

Southern Waters

Bill Page and I first crossed paths in March 1995 at the Maine Boatbuilders' Show, a pivotal event at which I also met Peter Chesworth and Jenny Bennett (see earlier chapters). An accomplished boatbuilder, a sailor, a former yacht broker, Bill is someone I probably wouldn't have gotten to know any other way. He's a "man of action," a restless spirit who fills his days with interesting experiences. I don't imagine he spends much time writing to addresses listed in little ads at the back of magazines. Fortunately, though, he's an avid show-goer—attending the ones with a large component of "salty" craft, as he puts it. He's always at the Maine Boatbuilders' and WoodenBoat shows, moving through the crowds on the lookout for interesting boats. Since I first met him, I've seen him at many other such events, talking to old friends and scrutinizing new boats.

Bill and I tossed around design ideas for a long time; our working relationship illustrates the tortuous path that design development sometimes takes.

At the Maine Boatbuilders' Show, Bill was thumbing through my catalog when he stopped at the sail plan for a boat I had named Rorqual. I had started the design in response to an inquiry from a Lake Erie sailor who was looking for a boat that could handle the lake's rough, short seas. Rorqual shared a page with the 20-foot pilot sloop Trooper—the first draft of the boat that ended up as Peter Chesworth's Indian Header (see Chapter 2). While Peter's boat still resembles Trooper, the variation of Rorqual I developed for Bill went through many changes.

When I first produce a cartoon for a design, it's been my custom to exaggerate the concept. It helps set the tone, and compromise comes later. This was true with Rorqual. If the design had proceeded, it would have evolved from this extreme version into a more useful,

Rorqual, an exaggerated cartoon of a double ender

moderate craft. As it was, the client lost interest, and the cartoon waited for someone else to pick up the trail. And that's just what Bill did. It wasn't long before I was sending him preliminary drawings incorporating changes he had suggested.

The Rorqual client had seemed especially interested in seaworthiness, at the expense of most other qualities, so I had drawn for him a boat based on the Block Island cowhorn and the closely related No Man's Land boats— double-enders, the former from 20 to 40 feet, the latter mostly around 18 to 22 feet. Since this was to be a trailered boat, I chose to keep the length just under 21 feet.

The challenge with a boat this size is getting a usable interior volume in the cabin. In the mid-1970s, I owned *Dawn Star*, a 1938-vintage Stone Horse, a Sam Crocker design. The raised deck on the boat seemed an ideal solution for this size range. A 30-footer has room under the side decks to sit upright below; the cabin trunk is there for standing headroom along the centerline, over the sole. At 21 feet, there isn't room to sit under the side decks, and the seats have to be pushed to the centerline to get sitting headroom. A raised deck alleviates the problem by taking the maximum headroom out to the sides.

The Stone Horse didn't have a skylight, and even though there was sufficient room to sit under the companionway, it was difficult to stand, even crouch, without opening the slide. I had designed Rorqual's unusual companionway/skylight in an attempt to remedy this problem. The inspiration came from a scuttle on a schooner I had seen wintering at Mystic Seaport Museum. It combined a companionway hatch with flanking skylights. The idea took some modifying, but I was able to combine the oversize companionway I had used on other designs, such as the Davies 18, with flanking skylights.

The rig was kept low and capable of drastic reduction, all on the theme of a heavy-weather boat.

The first thing that caught Bill's eye was that skylight hatchway. He thought it would be a good feature for a boat to trailer down to Florida, to cruise on "southern waters." By the time we were done, though, the boat had totally changed, and the skylights had been dropped. We had become concerned with their watertightness, and the difficulty of keeping the sun's hot vertical rays out of the interior.

Some time after Bill and I had been batting around these design ideas, I asked by letter if he would be interested in participating in a project for publication in this book. Reading a letter from Bill is like talking to him in person. He bowls you over with the strength of his enthusiasm.

"The answer is YES—LET'S DO IT!" Bill responded in his signature style, "I've got to think a bit more about just what I really want...; I expect it will be something along the lines of [what we've been discussing for] *Southern Waters* but just a little different here and there."

The Key West smackee from the Florida Keys came to mind as a possible prototype for the boat Bill was looking for. During the 1880s and 1890s, it was used in the inshore fisheries of southern Florida. I referred Bill to Howard Chapelle's lines and description of the *Jeff Brown* in the catalog of the Smithsonian Institution's National Watercraft Collection. The plans were taken off a half model in the collection as part of Chapelle's Works Progress Administration project that recorded the indigenous working craft of the United States.

A Rorqual draft leading toward a little pinky

The Key West smackee *Jeff Brown* was a typical example of the type. The boat's dimensions were close to what we were looking for: LOA 25 feet 3¼ inches, LOD 24 feet 3 inches, beam 8 feet 5½ inches, and a draft of 3 feet. Their rigs were similar to the Bahamian boats, with a low-aspect Bermudan main and a jib set to a bowsprit. There was no centerboard, and the rudderpost came up through the raked, heart-shaped transom.

I suggested we use this boat for inspiration. I felt that a 23-foot length and a draft of 2 feet 6 inches—with the addition of a centerboard—would be a good size for trailering, and I wanted to keep the displacement down to around 3,000 pounds. I sent Bill a Maxsurf printout of a proposed hull, a sail plan incorporating the skylights from Rorqual, and a few notes of explanation:

> The Key West smackees as a departure point have led to the proportions of the rig and the type of stem and transom. Beyond that, I also reconfigured the cabin so that the skylights are flat-topped, with the taper of the sides making up for the change in width as the cabin

Designer & Client

side follows the sheer in plan view.

I think that the proportions are starting to gel. The stern may appear a little high, but I think that is an illusion because the profile doesn't show the way the transom tucks in at the waterline. The shadow on the stern quarter will make sense of the sheer.

Let me know what you think.

I didn't need to worry on that score! Bill is not shy with his opinions:

First draft based on Rorqual cartoon

I appreciate your proposal drawings, which are very interesting, but here are some thoughts as to changes, and what I have in mind.

You may disagree with this, but I'd like the boat to be 27 feet minimum, or perhaps even 28 feet LOD, with an 8-foot 6-inch maximum beam—for trailerability from Maine to Florida. Draft of 2½ feet sounds fine. I'm sure the displacement will be appreciably over your suggested 3,000 pounds, but that's fine with me. I prefer a heavier boat, and I'll be hauling her on a very heavy-duty tandem-axle trailer with electric brakes; I'll tow with a yet-to-be-purchased one-ton truck with a powerful engine and drive train, conservatively rated for the job at hand, and I may "customize" the "rig" for camping out while en route.

I would like to base the design on the Key West smackee, as you suggested. I'd like a nearly plumb stem—almost straight, with just a little curve starting slightly above the waterline—and a well-raked transom with outboard rudder. I like flare in the deck forward, but with a fine entrance at the waterline. Also, please draw her with long, easy buttocks for a good, clean run that will move easily with good speed under power.

I'll plan on glued strip-cedar planking over laminated oak frames; for ease of construction, I'd like her keel to be "on edge" (vertical sides, but it can be tapered fore and aft if you think it best) rather than "built down," as shown in the sections of your computer drawings.

The boat has got to look salty. It needs a springy sheer with a good, high bow and a pleasing "tuck-up" at the stern, but please keep the sheer a bit lower aft in proportion than that shown on your drawing proposal. The skylight idea and revision will probably work out fine.

I would like the boat to sail well in light airs, and I'm presently thinking gaff-headed (with light spars) to get plenty of area without reaching for the sky. She's got to have a nice, long bowsprit with roller-furling/reefing genoa/jib, and of course it will be fitted with roller chocks for ease of handling my ever-trusty yachtsman's anchors.

Below, we'd like accommodations for only two—with the layout as open and spacious as possible. If it should work out that a quarter berth fits in without compromising the openness and spaciousness of the arrangement, that would be fine for the occasional overnight guest, and quarter berths usually make excellent stowage lockers on small boats.

I know we can't have full headroom in a boat of this size and retain the good looks we're after, but comfortable "lean-backs" for sitting headroom in the main cabin are a must.

A small diesel auxiliary would be my choice for power, but it's got to be located so I can get at any part of it without difficulty. I know that's often a hard one in a small boat, but we'll just have to slide it ahead and let the box become part of the companionway ladder if that's necessary for good access.

Bill didn't disappoint. He has definite ideas and laid them out cogently. I tried to pick up the trail. With my next set of drawings I sent along a copy of the drawing of the Key West smackee from Chapelle's catalog of the National Watercraft Collection and these thoughts:

On this draft, I've been quite faithful to the original in the hull form, except for the fuller line forward. As you can see, the main variance from your request is that the sternpost enters the transom at the waterline. I also drew a leg-o'-mutton Bermudan rig instead of a gaff. This is the rig used on the smackees, and it does give generous sail area without an overly tall mast. This stick is the same length as the one on the 23-footer in the previous cartoon. The mast can be fitted in a tabernacle.

I'm so glad you've gone toward a longer, heavier boat. People tend to put ease of trailering and launching ahead of performance afloat. It's good to see you put the emphasis where it belongs. After all, this isn't going to be a Winnebago. On a rough night out, the last thing on your mind will be how easy it was to back down the ramp.

The displacement stands at 8,400 pounds. As you can see in the body plan, the sections are quite full. We can shave off displacement if need be without taking away from the interior layout. I haven't drawn out the interior yet, but I feel confident that we can fit everything you've asked for. I wanted you to have a look at the profile before getting too carried away.

The sail area/displacement ratio is 21.5. This is high, reflecting the full area of the genoa. Furling it down to 100 square feet brings the ratio down to 17.6. You specify good performance in light airs. This rig should give it to you. By easing the outhaul on the loose-footed main, the sail can be powered up for light air. The big genoa will do its share. A topsail, similar to the ones used on the Chesapeake log canoes, can be fitted as well. It's like a Sunfish sail set on a yard and boom that is set from the deck.

This rig won't point very high, but its performance should match that of the hull in this regard. A gaff rig might do a bit better to windward, especially if it is peaked quite high. The Key sponge boats used a gaff sloop rig that provides a precedent for using it on a smackee. My feeling is that the 10-hp diesel will make up for any shortcomings. On a reach, I think this boat will go. The same goes for speed under power. I hope you like the way the run is shaping up.

There should be plenty of room around the engine. It will go aft of the centerboard case under a bridge deck. There will be access from above and also from the quarter berths and the back of the cabin. The only restriction will be the 4-inch-wide centerboard case ahead of it, but this shouldn't present a problem.

Actually, while we're at the centerboard, I should note that the original smackees had 3-foot draft on 28 feet without a board. This might be an option worth considering. The long, "on-edge" keel with a bit more drop at its heel will give an adequate lateral plane without the complication of the centerboard and case. Of course, this further complicates trailering for the faint of heart, if not for you. And, it does add 6 inches to your draft in an area where that can be a significant difference. It's just a thought....

Before I wrap up, there is only one real disagreement that I have with your specifications. I don't like the laminated oak frames. First off, I'm assuming lamination with epoxy. Oak and epoxy don't get along. You may have intended resorcinol, which will glue oak very well, but it is more difficult to use and adds another set of mixing bowls to the pantry. I would rather see epoxy used throughout.

Let me just say that it is a lot easier for me to be pounding this "advice" out on my keyboard and mailing it off. I don't think I'd be so brash with my "construction tips" if I had to deliver them to you in person. I wouldn't be able to discount your years of experience so easily.

The house is similar to what I've shown you before. The main difference is that the central section carrying the companionway slide also supports the forehatch. This hatch is hinged and not sliding—which takes it off the foredeck. The ports are round, and the forward one is smaller than the other two.

I hope the stem curve approaches your ideal. I appreciate your very strong tastes regarding the boat's profile. Perhaps the best way to deal with it would be for you to trace your idea over this drawing and send me the tracing. Then I can incorporate it into the next drawing.

The next step, if you agree with the overall parameters shown in these drawings, is to produce a draft of the interior and a revised profile and sail plan. If this is too far from what you had in mind, then rein me in and I'll draw another cartoon.

Specifically, I need to know how you feel about the displacement (the current displacement gives us a healthy ballast ratio), the choice of rig, centerboard or 3-foot draft, and the overall look of the profile and cabin.

Bill's response was, as usual, direct:

Now we're getting somewhere. A real sweet and salty boat is emerging....

First, some comments regarding some minor changes I've sketched in on the drawings.

- Most important: I've sketched in the anchor to rough scale for a 30- to 35-pounder and moved the roller chock to about 40 inches forward of the stems; these anchors have about 36-inch shank length in this size. I think I got the larger anchor on her just in time—she was dragging ashore fast, with sharp ledges to leeward, with the "lunch hook" you had drawn....
- How about a more interesting tiller with a little reverse curve?
- I think I'd like to give up on the skylight/cabin-roof idea. I'm too afraid of leaks when driving to windward. Also, we can then give the trunk/roofline a little sweep—up toward the forward end as I've drawn—much prettier to my eye. Next, the continuous riser I can't

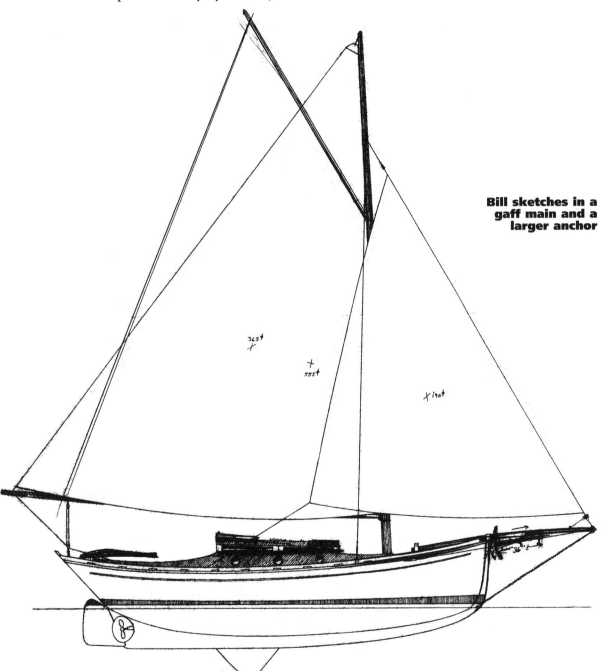

Bill sketches in a gaff main and a larger anchor

Designer & Client

deal with—doesn't look right. Let's make a well-tapered main hatch riser—nice and high aft but "wicked" low forward, as per sketch, with nice ogee at forward end. A separate hatch forward is fine and can be hinged.

- I like the sheer very much, but I think the quick rise way forward is too much. I don't want to lower the height at the stem, so I'd suggest easing the curve aft a bit through stations 2 to 8+. See what you think—I roughed in my idea.
- I've straightened the stem a whisker and hardened the knuckle above the waterline just a mite. Also, let's straighten the rabbet line toward the stemhead so the exposed wood tapers down nicely as we near the sheer.
- I really think I'd like to have her gaff-headed with a shorter boom with less overhang. I penciled in a quick rough sketch. I'm thinking light spars (including gaff), and I think it will be a more efficient and easier-handling sail than the long-boomed, short-hoist marconi main.
- I think you're right that we ought to ease up the displacement just a little. Can we perhaps give her just a little more deadrise by raising the bilges and perhaps hardening up the turn, and making her a little narrower at the waterline (I'm assuming you've given her the maximum beam of 8 feet 6 inches at the sheer) so we retain a bit of flare in the topsides until way aft to station 19 or 20? I like the idea of the reserve stability that flare provides when starting to heel; I like the looks; and it's much better when going alongside pilings, which are prevalent in southern waters. A slight reverse toward the rabbet at the transom would be pretty, and I'd harden the turn up at the transom as well.
- I like her plan/waterline views and the profile/buttocks, except I wonder if the upward curvature of the buttocks aft (stations 15+ to 19+) could be eased just a little. They seem real sweet with a nice, long run but then head "uphill" rather quickly toward the transom—to my eye, at least. But this I want to leave entirely up to you, for you know far more about proper underwater hull design than I.

I think I'd prefer to stay with the 2½-foot draft and give her a centerboard rather than going to 3-foot draft with full keel. This will make her more easily trailerable, *and* I expect she will be a better performer to windward. I am wondering, though—is the board, as shown, large enough? It seems small to me, but again, you're the doctor. For my part, however, I'd rather have it a bit large and not put her down all the way if not needed.

I guess that covers about all my thoughts—for the moment, at least.... I like the overall shape and theme of the boat very much. She is going to be a "keeper."

P.S. Regarding the frames: I'm thinking of two layers only - outer layer about one-third of total frame molding and inner layer two-thirds. Might glue them and might not—with the one-third/two-thirds idea, the planking screws will get a good hold on the inner layer. That's what is really important. In my own *Mimi Rose*—and, for that matter, in all of [Gordon] Swift's and [Bud] McIntosh's boats—the frames are half the molded thickness each layer, but with

126

copper rivets through to sandwich the whole thing together. I think screws would be better on this lighter-displacement boat, thus the one-third/two-thirds frame. Also, at this point I'm not sure at all that I even want to cover her with 'glass/epoxy sheathing. From what I've seen lately, I think it may give more trouble than it's worth. Many boats have been simply strip-built over frames, with excellent, long-lasting results. George Luzier's boats in Sarasota, Florida, are a proven example; also Farnham Butler's on Mount Desert Island [Maine].

We leave the "sky-light" cabin top behind

The Controversy [by Farnham Butler] is another example of the type, except most of these are lighter displacement and without frames—structural bulkheads only. But Farnham Butler's own 37-foot yawl *Constellation* still looks almost like new—after nearly a half-century of sailing. I would, however, prefer to bend-in frames on this boat for added strength. And, of course, I always like rugged floor timbers, which spread out well away from the keel, and then securely fasten the planking to the floors as well as the frames.

I've chosen strip/composite as the "default" construction method for most of my designs because I think it best serves the "average" contemporary wooden-boat owner. It is relatively easy for an amateur to use and is able to handle the dry/wet cycles without damage. A superior boat can be built using traditional methods, however. If the skill and the proper materials are available, and the boat can be maintained at a traditional yard, there are many designs that will be built best of solid timber without glues and cloth sheathing. Bill Page (who recently retired) and Gordon Swift (who may never retire) have been among the best builders in the country for this kind of construction.

When I had revised drawings ready for Bill, I sent them along with my reactions to his comments/requests:

> The longer cabin is the logical thing to do. At the beginning of a design based on a traditional type, it's tempting to keep elements of the design similar to the prototype. At this point, it's time to adjust the elements for practicality.
>
> On larger boats, I like to break up the interior a bit to provide private spaces. On this boat, I agree with you that the more open the interior is, the bigger and airier the boat will feel. I like to use structural bulkheads instead of molds to set up the hull. This boat should be built on molds so that the bulkheads can be kept to a minimum.
>
> We can fit quarter berths as you've suggested. It would be nice to

have the head enclosed, but since your overriding concern is for an open layout, the head under the V-berth will be the best solution.

I continued working on the plans and eventually forwarded the latest, including the interior layout, to Bill. He replied, directly of course:

> I think the layout is good except for one thing that I believe will not work well at all. That is where you've located the sink—tucked in under the bridge deck. You can't get your head in there to see what you're doing. I'm also puzzled about the diagonally positioned opening on the starboard counter. Is that the ice chest?? [This was my attempt to show a chart lying on the chart table; you can't win them all.] Anyway, I think the sink has *got* to go in the starboard galley counter, with a small ice chest *if* possible. If not, then we'll have to use a portable ice chest somehow. At least food and dish and cooking-pot lockers can be worked into the starboard side next to the sink and also into the athwartship (where the sink is now) counter area under the bridge deck. Stowage bins and areas of this sort are ultra-important for happy cruising. I gather we get at the engine through an opening aft of the companionway ladder?
>
> I think she'll be a "good little ship," Tony, and I look forward to hearing your ideas re the above.

Then one more note arrived to remind me of the last point of contention:

> *Please* draw the sink on the *starboard side* with the ice chest, *if* there is room. Otherwise, the ice chest (or a portable one) could go aft of the ladder under the bridge deck.

After this, Bill's boat went back into the rotation of designs, and months went by during which I worked on other projects. Finally I got back to *Southern Waters* and worked up the final set of drawings. But, as will be seen, I managed to perpetuate the sink/ice-chest controversy.

> I've enclosed the final lines plan, accommodation plan, and sail plan, along with a sail plan for an offshoot of the design, which we might call *Northern Waters*. I couldn't resist drawing an alternate rig, and I thought it was a good opportunity to show a deep-draft cruising version as well. Between the two versions, there are enough options to satisfy many tastes. For instance, one could combine the shoal hull with the long cabin, or the deep hull and the gaff rig, etc.
>
> In the same spirit of adventure, I've ignored your request, stressed in your last letter, to move the sink from under the bridge deck. As my three-year-old friend Jimmy Miller says, "Don't you be mad at me." When it comes to actual construction, it's a simple matter to locate the sink to starboard as you requested. I've kept it under the bridge deck to leave room for a good-size icebox to starboard. The icebox could go under the bridge deck, but it would be right next to the engine heat. The changes I've made to the height and depth of the sink counter should leave plenty of room to see and work at the sink from a fold-down seat on the side of the companionway ladder.

The long house shown on the *Northern Waters* sail plan would
resolve the galley question, as well as improve access to the quarter
berths. With the long house, the cockpit seats are still long enough
to sleep on. I think it comes down to whether you want to cruise two
and daysail a crowd, or cruise two-plus and daysail four.

The rest of the interior shouldn't have any surprises. I've kept the
centerboard on the small side so that the case won't intrude too
much. It's an efficient foil shape and should provide plenty of lift.
The board is made of a galvanized steel core with lead cast around
it and sheathed in glass and epoxy. It provides almost 600 pounds of

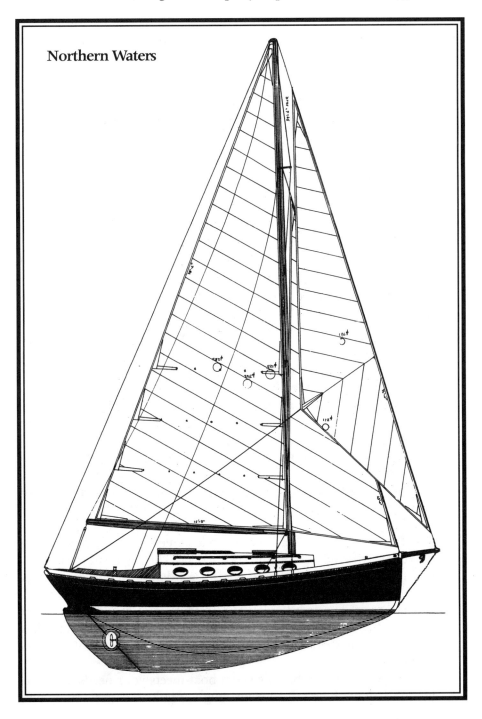

Northern Waters

ballast. Along with 2,400 pounds in a lead shoe, this gives us a 41 percent ballast/displacement ratio.

Regarding centerboards, there is a trade-off in the choice of which type to use. The traditional low-aspect, more-or-less-triangular board is an inefficient foil. It works by area alone, without much lift. The drawback also includes a higher wetted surface, and this type is more intrusive on the interior accommodation. The benefit is that it can be raised and lowered partway without much effect on helm balance.

A much smaller foil can give better pointing ability, but only at speeds and angles of attack that allow it to achieve lift and not stall. A boat with a foil board must be sailed differently, especially in light air. When tacking, or coming up to windward, it is necessary to build up way before attempting to point high. The foil can then develop a good flow and build up lift. If the boat is pinched, the board will stall and lose all effect, whereas a larger, flat-plate centerboard would still provide some resistance to side force. If this caveat is followed, then the advantages of the foil can be exploited fully: less wetted surface, active lift to windward, and less intrusion on the interior.

In strong winds, the board is lifted partway, which seems counterintuitive, but the result is that the center of resistance moves aft, and up. This counteracts the increased weather helm created by heeling and also reduces the height of the lever arm between center of resistance and effort. This has an effect similar to reefing sail: lessening the heeling moment.

My comments for Bill accompanying the final plans continued:

The rig is large. It's intended to provide adequate area for light air without the need for further light-air sails. The roller-reefing jib can be rolled into working jib size. Before there were auxiliary engines, mainsails were sized for light air. The first short reef corresponds to a post-auxiliary mainsail.

It's only natural for me to want to draw a counterpart to your boat for sunny climes. For me, every design leads to another, and then another. Every design is a set of compromises based on a certain set of assumptions. If we alter those assumptions, the result will change to suit.

Northern Waters is a boat for cold, green seas with deep channels between seaweed-covered rock ledges. The rig is tall for light air and for working to windward against a tide, but it can be snugged way down. I haven't gone into the interior. We'll leave that for another time. The *Southern Waters* interior will fit, of course, with improved access to the quarter berths and headroom in the galley. (There's more than 6-foot headroom throughout, thanks to the deeper draft.)

I hope you agree that the shoal boat meets your needs. I can see you aboard at the end of a sparkling winter's day, with an awning spread over the long cockpit and your "fisherman" anchor planted in white sand under crystalline, turquoise *Southern Waters*.

Bill's reaction arrived a few weeks later.

All is well and *everything* looks just fine—except we will move that sink to the starboard side and the icebox under the bridge deck "when we build her in Heaven".... Thanks very much for everything.

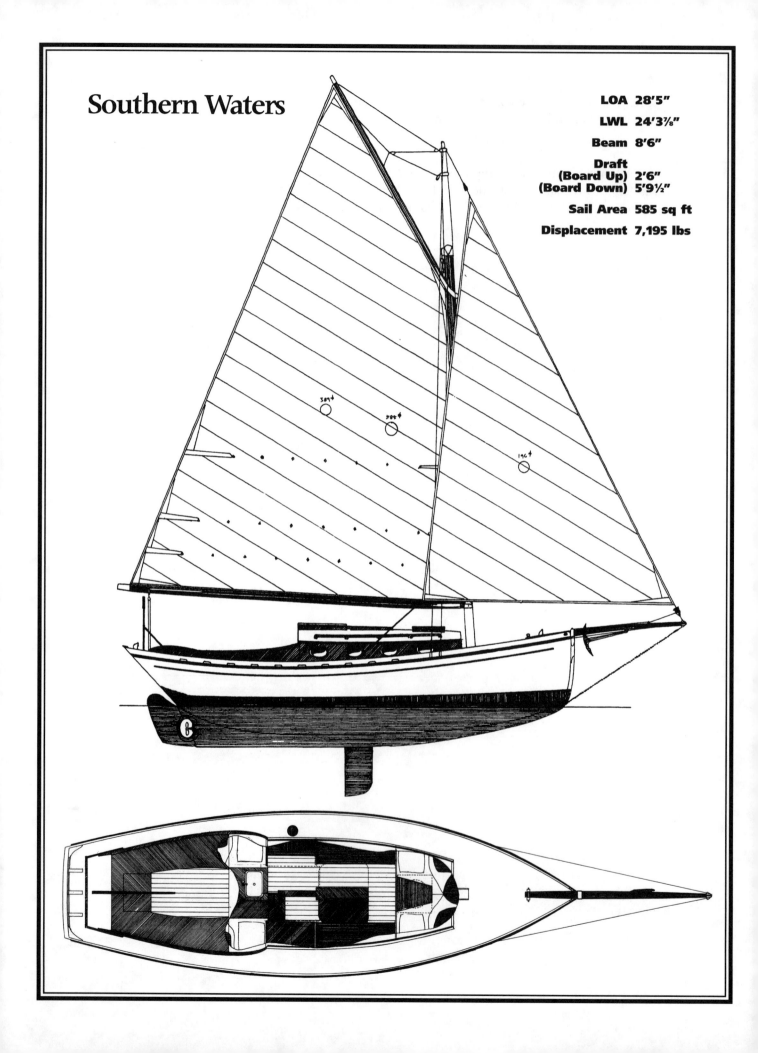

Southern Waters

LOA 28'5"

LWL 24'3⅞"

Beam 8'6"

Draft
(Board Up) 2'6"
(Board Down) 5'9½"

Sail Area 585 sq ft

Displacement 7,195 lbs

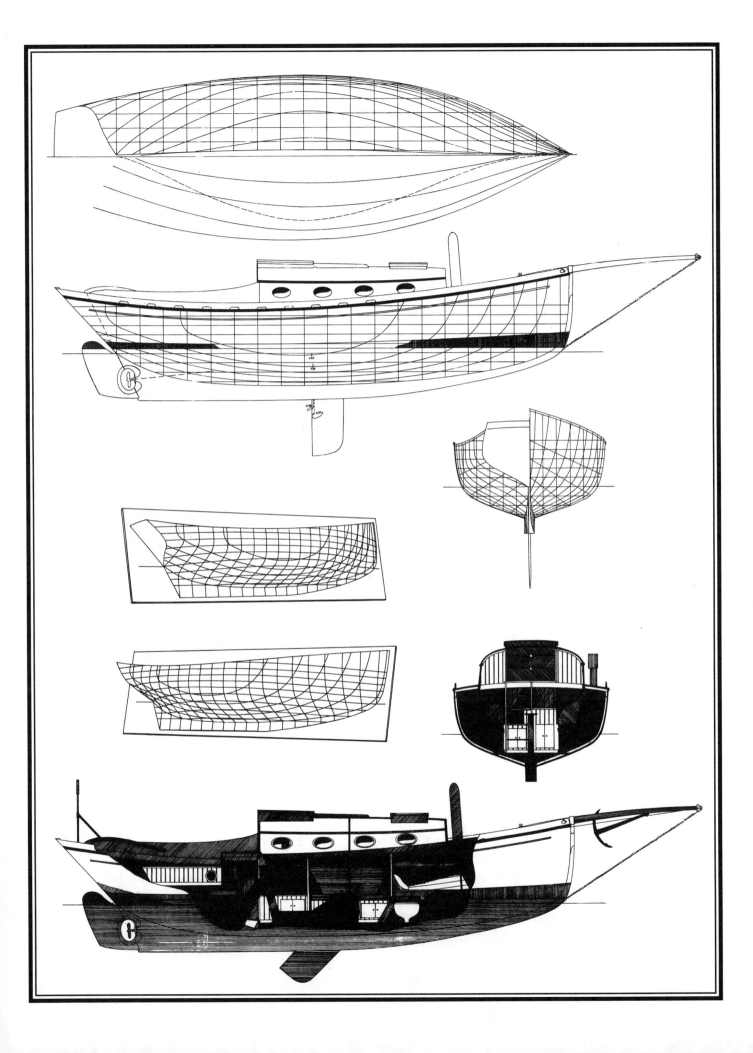

CHAPTER 8

The Double Headsail Sloop

Gordon Swift—Swifty to all who know him—is a boatbuilder in southern New Hampshire. His shop and house are situated in rolling farm country some miles from the shore. At first glance, his place looks like many old New England farms—until you notice all the sailboats stored in his yard. He and his wife, Doris, have lived there for more than 40 years, raising a family and building a lot of boats over that time.

Many of us who are interested in traditional boats, and are now in our forties, have tried to keep alive certain values from the past. But we've had to imagine and study about that past to achieve our goal—much of what we have tried to honor had already passed before we came of age. Fortunately for all of us, Gordon is a bridge to the best traditions of New England boatbuilding.

It would be easy to say that Swifty is "old" if you just read his birthdate; he's in his seventies. A pleasant confusion arises when you meet him, especially in his shop surrounded by his work. He's of medium build, wiry, and strong. His eyes are pale blue, and he has a wild shock of hair. Physical and mental energy just boil off him, like wisps of vapor off a rocket booster sitting on the launch pad.

As with a rocket ready for blastoff, you just know better than to get between Swifty and his work. We were lucky enough to see him on a slow day, when he was well into building a 36-foot Sam Crocker cutter. The hull filled his shop, the cabintop up among the rafters. Swifty was once again combining building with instruction. Over the years, he has taken on a number of apprentices, just as he himself had apprenticed with the legendary New Hampshire boatbuilder Bud McIntosh many years ago.

The owner of the cutter—a strapping, operatic-looking fellow in his thirties, a professional deep-sea diver who's twice Swifty's size in every dimension—was working alongside him on the project. In one of those situations now codified under the catchphrase "win-win"—common when people of goodwill meet each other with generosity of spirit—this young man was getting not only a Swift boat but also an education in boatbuilding and life. A bargain price for taking the opportunity to learn.

Gordon showed us a photo album of the Crocker's construction, starting with the pit dug in the shop floor to cast the 10,000-pound keel in place. Standing there under the loom of the hull, we got to the picture of the hull careened on its side for "dubbing off"—the hand planing of carvel planking that's the first step to a smooth, fair skin. In his impatience to get on with the job, 150-pound, 70-year-old Swifty had dubbed off both sides of the hull in a matter of days while "the young fella" was off on a diving job.

I well remember dubbing off a 22-foot Friendship sloop when I was 24 years old. Eric Dow and I each took a side. With much of the work done at arm's length and above shoulder height, the jack plane was soon torture to wield. It took us—two of us in our early twenties—more time to smooth that 22-footer than it took the 70-year-old Swifty to do his 36-footer. The math on this comparison gets complicated. Not only does a boat's surface area grow exponentially with length, but how does one compare the human factors involved in such an equation?

One could be in awe of Swifty as a result of his accomplishments alone, but beyond that, he's a gentleman—in the full meaning the term had years ago. He's an example to us all for the way he and Doris have put together a life, coupling accomplishment with affection and dignity.

Gordon and Bill Page (see previous chapter) have been friends for many years, and it was through Bill that I met Gordon. Shortly afterwards, I ran into the Swifts in Brooklin, Maine, when they were on their annual August cruise. I was rowing around of an evening, admiring the collection of boats that grace the anchorage off *WoodenBoat* magazine's headquarters, when one boat caught my eye—a double-headsail sloop of about 25 feet. There was some Crocker to her, and something else.... As I rowed, the owner came on deck for a look. It was Gordon, and he invited me aboard. This was his boat, *Madrigal of Exeter*. Of course. How could I have missed it?

We went below and sat in the glow of the setting sun, which has a strong orange tint on those late summer evenings along the coast of Maine. We talked about the boat and how their cruise had been. I would have talked about anything to prolong the peace and serenity of the moment. We didn't know each other well enough to just sit there and bask, although the sense of their welcome had me laid out on the settee. The shaft of light from the port over Doris's head streamed in and occasionally flared in my eyes....

Not long afterward I offered to design a boat for the Swifts to be included in this book, and they accepted. Gordon then sent me a hand-written list of particulars. He's never long-winded, preferring to say just what is necessary to get on with the job:

- A sloop rig, mast stepped on deck in a tabernacle. Four-foot draft with a full-length cast-iron keel, all ballast outside. A waterline of 23 to 24 feet and an overall length of 28 or 29 feet.
- A bowsprit with accommodation for anchors and roller-furling jib. Boomkin for backstay—economically sound, and you don't have to pay for the extra length.
- An outboard rudder with tiller, no counter stern.
- Footwell cockpit using deck for seats. A gallows frame.
- Diesel engine, about 20 gallons of fuel. Steel tank sandblasted and epoxied.
- Below, an enclosed head forward with minimum holding tank.
- Headroom could be 5 feet 10 inches.
- Two bunks with a possibility of two more for not more than two or three nights.
- Two-burner propane stove with oven, Force 10 propane heater.
- Forty gallons of water. No pressure system, hand pumps only (from Fynspray?).
- Icebox with minimum of 3 inches of insulation; no drain, only a pumpout.
- I would expect this boat to have close to a 10-foot beam, therefore quarter berths should not be ruled out. They can be used for storage when not being slept in.
- I might as well identify myself as being "old school," but cedar-on-oak with copper rivets is still the way I would want to build this boat. My only concession to modern technology would be plywood decks covered with fiberglass.
- Should you come up with a much better design using cold molding, I would have to take that into consideration. Economic concerns, especially at our age, create demands and limitations, so like every other boat, we are talking about compromise.
- The additional length over *Madrigal* is to try to get to windward a little better in a chop.

•If you should need any more information, please let me know, but I have to get this off while it is five below zero and I cannot bring myself to go to the shop.

I had been excited by the prospect of Swifty's commission. What would it be? I had shown him a 40-foot dragger-yacht design that I'd done based on the eastern-rigged draggers of Provincetown, common in my youth. He'd been interested in the boat when we visited him. But I was neither surprised nor disappointed when his letter outlined a boat similar to *Madrigal*, only a little larger. Here was a chance to learn from his many years of experience with the type. It was also a lesson in modesty. It's easy to get carried away, asking for too much boat, too much flash. Here he was showing me the importance of the basics: a modest cruising boat for a couple, in a type developed through the first half of this century. My task was to reinterpret this familiar recipe and perhaps bring up to date some elements of construction and equipment.

I did some preliminary work on the design and sent Gordon Maxsurf-generated prints of the hull, plus accommodation and sail plans, adding a few comments:

First presentation

> I couldn't help but start with my own vague ideas of what your new boat might be like. I used your specifications wherever they applied, but I took my desire to draw a clipper-bowed boat as inspiration for the profile.
>
> The rig has double headsails. The boat will balance with either the working jib or the roller-furling genoa. The sails would only be flown together wing-and-wing in light airs, or perhaps on a broad reach. The genoa will need to be furled to tack easily, but this is preferable to having to walk it around anyway. The working jib could also roller-furl with the addition of an outhaul to the jibboom.

Even with all Gordon's experience and knowledge, I couldn't resist my habit of starting the preliminary cartoon with a more or less willful departure from the specifications given to me. I tend to do this for two reasons. First, it gives me a chance to stretch my imagination. If held too closely in check by trying to follow directions, I find the result at this early stage is usually stultified. The other reason is to challenge the owner to explain his or her reasons for choosing a certain type. This is my chance to contribute something that might jostle the owner's perceptions of what they're after, and let them see the boat in their mind's eye from a slightly different perspective. The new input will either show them something intriguing that wins them over, or give them all the more reason to stick to their guns, having had to defend them against my heresies.

I continued my explanation to Gordon:

This rig is versatile without requiring much foredeck work or any additional light sails. The displacement now stands at 9,600 pounds. On a 23-foot 5½-inch LWL, the boat has a displacement/length ratio of 332, in the low end of the heavy range. The working jib and main have an area of 427 square feet, for a sail area/displacement ratio of 15.1, considered moderate. The genoa and main have an area of 567 square feet, for a sail area/displacement ratio of 20, a high value.

L. Francis Herreshoff's H-28 has a displacement/length ratio of 325, on a 9,017-pound displacement and 23-foot 1½-inch LWL. The sail area is only 343 square feet in the ketch rig, giving the boat a sail area/displacement ratio of 12.7, considered quite low. While I haven't yet worked out a ballast weight, it is bound to be higher than the 31 percent ratio (in the low moderate range) of the H-28. We also have here a beam of 8 feet on the waterline, as opposed to 7 feet 4 inches, and an overall beam of 10 feet versus 8 feet 9 inches The 4-foot draft is 6 inches greater than that of the H-28 as well, all adding power to carry more sail. Combined with the more efficient sloop rig, as opposed to the ketch, I think we should have a boat that should be both faster overall and better to windward in particular.

Not to pick on the H-28, but I thought it would be a good trial horse, since it was meant to meet a similar mission as a wholesome cruiser for two. In this design, we also have 6 feet 3 inches of headroom (versus 4 feet 8 inches under the coach roof) and two more permanent berths.

Arrangements, first presentation

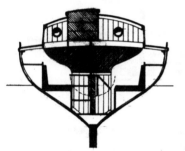

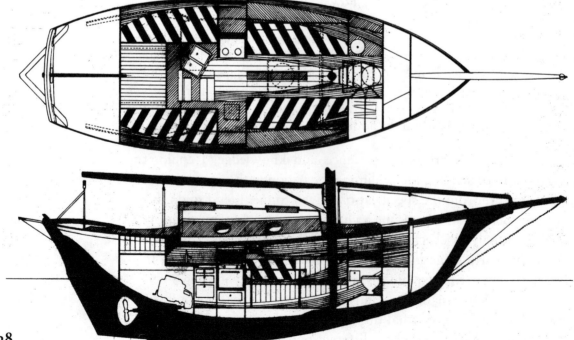

You asked for 5 feet 10 inches of headroom. Of course, we can lower the coach roof to match that, but I prefer to draw boats that I can stand up in. If standing headroom is intended, then 6 feet 3 inches is the minimum I like to use.

The engine shown is a 2-cylinder, 18-hp Yanmar with a V- drive. This keeps the engine out of the cabin. It has good access by removing the companionway steps and taking out part of the bulkhead and countertop. These can be made to fit together with sliding bolts to facilitate their removal. Fuel tanks will be on either side of the engine.

Water tanks can be fitted under the settee/berths in the saloon. A small tank can also be built into the table base. The holding tank is forward of the head, under the sail bin. A propane tank can be stored in a compartment built up against the transom with vents to drain any leak overboard. This compartment should be fiberglassed to ensure that its bottom is airtight inboard. The cabin heater can be mounted on the aft side of the mast.

The quarter berths are full-size. They do have limited headroom, but they should be comfortable in a seaway. Access requires a bit of athleticism. I think they'll politely nudge guests off the boat after a few nights. They'll be great for storage. Strategically placed deck prisms, and perhaps opening ports into the cockpit well, would go far to make them more comfortable.

A bit more on the rig. At midboom, the main is sheeted to a traveler on the aft edge of the bridge deck. Along with the vang, this allows much more precise control of the sail than the older style of sheet. The boom is a little long to rely on a solid vang to take the place of a topping lift, so a lift is shown. No battens are shown, but the sail would need them to support its deep roach. Running backstays also would be a good idea.

Please mark up the duplicate prints with your thoughts. I especially want your input into the scantlings you prefer to use for the hull, so notes on frame dimensions, spacing, stringers, shelf and clamp, etc., would be greatly appreciated. From my point of view, this is also an opportunity to learn from your experience.

Then came Swifty's reaction:

Thank you for the set of lines for the 28-foot 9-inch sloop. It is always a difficult period when you submit plans to new owners, having been there many times with other designers. At this point in time, you may wonder if you can ever satisfy their desires.

The following may sound like criticism but hopefully will be suggestions so we can both be satisfied with the end result.

I would like to see less deadrise and round out the bilge. I am enclosing pictures of our current boat showing roundness of bilge and large transom. I think this could be done without jeopardizing speed but would increase room inside. Our fat little pot can at times do 6 knots.

The nice hollow forward should make her go to windward nicely; with a larger transom, it might help flatten out the buttock lines and add room below.

Your 6-foot-plus headroom is nice, but we would be happy with

6 feet, period. The slight reduction in height by lifting the cabin sole would make more room.

One thing must be remembered in designing a boat under 200 feet—that everything is a compromise.

I would prefer that the house continue forward to where you have the forward coaming terminating. This would put the hatch up where it would not be sitting in a puddle if taking a wave over the bow. Having done this, you can have a track on the housetop for the staysail so it will lead back along the house and keep the foredeck clear.

I would like to see the mast raised a foot and end in a tabernacle. A compression post of course would be necessary; it would eliminate leaks around the mast and give one the ability to raise and lower at will.

Having jacked the whole rig up a foot gives room for a dodger and also close to 6-foot headroom under the boom. Having the mainsheet on the bridge deck can be dangerous and, like a sore thumb, always on hand. I would like to see the bridge deck 6 inches wider by moving the aft end of the cockpit a foot to make it 3 feet 6 inches long and making the footwell only 2 feet wide.

Let's move the gallows frame forward and put the mainsheet on the aft end of the boom.

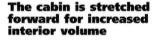

The cabin is stretched forward for increased interior volume

Please turn the engine around. There is room enough if you raise the shaft line. V-drives are not for me, and with the sound insulation available, noise wouldn't be the problem in a wooden boat that it would be in fiberglass. A 2-cylinder Universal or Westerbeke would be a good job.

One other thought comes to mind. Is it possible to move the staysail aft another foot? The loss of sail area would be minimal and might provide room enough for the genoa to come through without our having to go forward to pass it through. I think 2 ft. would work.

I believe I've given you enough food for thought for a while. I remember one boat I built to Joel White's design and how many preliminary plans went by the board before a final plan was achieved.

Thank you for your patience and understanding.

At a meeting with Bill Page not long after this, Bill mentioned that he had the impression that Swifty was probably holding back his true preferences concerning the clipper bow, so I wrote to Swifty:

At the risk of annoying you with my second guesses, I hope that you feel comfortable to make whatever comments or criticisms you need to regarding this design. I truly want this to be your design in the sense that this is the boat you would build if the circumstances were appropriate.... It's my job to help facilitate the creation of the client's wishes, and not to dictate them, especially when the client has so much more experience than I do, and from whom I hope to learn much in the process.

Time passed. After prodding Gordon with another letter, I finally got an answer. There was an explanation for the delay ("no rest for the wicked") and, always concise and to the point, the message: "Please remove the clipper bow."

That made it official, so the clipper bow went. Some time later, after I had sent reworked drawings, Swifty wrote again, suggesting a few other changes:

> I am happy to hear that you are getting up to speed with your new Maxsurf program, because I have made a small change. I like an open taffrail so that water, dirt, etc., can pass right out. It also gives the boomkin easy passage. I am afraid I mutilated the sheerline in the profile [drawing], trying to show what I have in mind, but I think you can get the idea. Don't think it will destroy the looks of the boat at all.
>
> I wonder what you will think about what I did to the rudder? My feeling is that putting the addition on the bottom gives you much better control; of course, there will be only a slight sensation of weather helm.

**The clipper bow
removed**

When the design for Swifty's boat came back to the top of the pile, I completed the next round of drawings and sent them off to him with some explanatory notes:

> Let me take you through the new drawings. The changes are really minimal from the last set. The larger scale of the drawings just brings out the details. The two quarter berths are aft, and accessible from the platform over the engine. The one to port, behind the galley sink, is for use as a last resort—by an agile, small person—but the other is easy enough to get into. For normal cruising with just two people, these berths are just for storage anyway.
>
> The cockpit seats are at deck level and will have hatches into storage spaces inboard of the quarter berths and in the lazarette. A bridge-deck hatch reaches the storage space behind the companionway steps. The footwell is self-bailing. The seats are large enough to sleep on. The stern rail is open, as you suggested, and the boomkin legs come in over the deck.
>
> The engine platform can be used as a seat when working in the galley. The gimbaled stove is to port, with crockery lockers out-

board. To starboard is the chart table, with an icebox under it. There's a locker outboard here as well—for books and any electronics. I've shown the port berth made up and the starboard one as a seat. They provide comfortable seating for up to four at the folding table. A curtain separates the head from the cabin.

The compression of the mast is carried by the head bulkhead aft and the large hanging knees just forward of the mast. The berths extend under the counters each side of the head. I've maintained 6-foot 2-inch headroom below. It can be reduced by raising the sole and/or lowering the coach roof if you prefer less height. I wanted to maintain the option for taller guys like me to stand upright.

The large forepeak can be reached through the forward bulkhead from the head. It will be the primary sail storage area and have a chain locker below. Waste tanks, with a 25-gallon capacity, are under the sole. The fuel and freshwater tanks are outboard of the engine, under the quarter berths, with 40 gallons each. The batteries are either side of the engine. Ballast is 3,700 pounds of cast iron.

The interior is unusual, but it does provide a private head and four berths. The boat could be laid out in a more conventional style, with a double berth forward and settees amidship, etc.

Swifty's next letter summarized his perceptions of the design, and it covered some changes he thought he'd still like to see. Some of these are reconsiderations of his original specifications:

We both know that no matter how big a boat gets, it still winds up being a compromise. The hull I like; I realize you liked the clipper bow, but I like the spoon bow better. To me, a clipper bow belongs on a Friendship or a skipjack.

It may be the McIntosh influence [Swift was greatly influenced by the late designer/boatbuilder Bud McIntosh], but the nice hollow in the bow looks great. I am sure it helps a small boat like this when punching to windward in a chop.

Diagonals and buttocks are nice and fair. She should slide along nicely. All the specifications indicate that it will speak well for itself under all conditions. Most of all, the lines are pleasing to the eye, which is very important from a builder's point of view. Most people today would not be impressed, but we are not looking for a speedboat. We want one that will take us both ways, out and back, in comfort.

The rudderhead will have to be raised above the taffrail in order for the tiller to have free movement in a vertical plane so as not to impede access to a hatch forward of the transom.

In the cockpit area, I would like not to have a hatch in the bridge deck and make this area accessible from inside. Lift-up seats are fine, but I would put an opening port in each side of the footwell, and possibly in the forward end. I definitely want a hatch aft of the cockpit. This is always a place where visual inspection is nice, especially as the boat gets older; it's also handy for docklines, fenders, etc. The stove in the galley for me will be propane. Somewhere in all these lockers, I will find a place for a gas-tight propane locker.

I had mentioned the propane locker in a letter to Gordon, but I hadn't shown it in the accommodations plan I sent. The locker will be similar to the ones on other designs in this book, with a vent out through the transom.

Swifty continued:

> Your comment about quarter berths on a boat this size usually winding up as storage is absolutely right. They have become that on our current boat. The fact remains that they are available as berths if needed, even if only for a weekend. They do make great storage.
>
> At the risk of being too critical, check the alignment of the shaft log and the engine. As drawn, it would be quite hard to make it work in reality. Could be changed, though, when the lines are on the floor.
>
> Six-foot-two is very nice headroom, and a demand I am sure you will find most everyone wants. At the risk of cutting down the resale value, I would be tempted to raise the cabin sole 2 inches so as not to have to walk uphill on the ceiling so much but still have 6 feet 2 inches in way of the hatches. With someone of Doris's and my stature, it would be fine to have only 6 feet under the beams.
>
> Should we keep this interior as drawn, I would think a 2-inch brass or stainless pipe at the forward end of the table would help in supporting the mast tabernacle.
>
> With the hull complete and the ceiling inside, we would be confronted with the "what if" syndrome. With most every boat I have had the pleasure of building, I have been confronted with "what if." As a result, the original interior usually winds up being something other than drawn.

Swifty's suggested changes to the final drawings

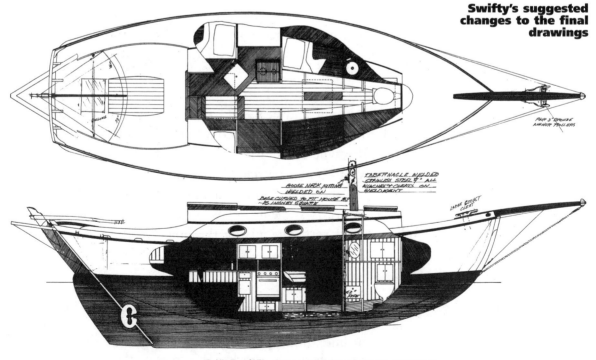

I HAVE USED THIS METHOD OF MAST STEPPING ON EVERY BOAT I HAVE BUILT. WORK WELL WITH EITHER WOOD OR ALUMINUM.

In the matter of mast support, I had shown a compression post in the earlier drafts. Now I've made the head bulkhead carry the load to improve access forward.

As is the case with all of these designs, I agree wholeheartedly that the interior should be reconsidered once the hull is built. There's no other way to take full advantage of the flexibility of a custom boat than to perform a final "fitting" at that point. But you do need to have a practical interior in mind from the design stage. It gives you a fall-back position and will troubleshoot the hull dimensions to make sure that something usable can be done there. Beyond that, depending on how much the interior is tied to the hull's framework (with integral bulkheads, for instance), the layout should be mocked up before the commitment is made.

Swifty continued:

> As much as I like cast-iron ballast, I would think long and hard about perhaps using lead. When we built John Noon's Crocker 36 and we had it laid out on the floor, I kept the same profile, but I substituted lead for iron, for the simple reason that we could pour our own lead keel and there is only one place left in New England that will pour iron of that magnitude. The cost saving is considerable.

Swifty had requested iron in his first letter, but in fact, I've always preferred to specify lead. First it is denser, and most important, as Swifty brought up, it is much more readily cast, either commercially or on-site by the builder. It can be melted with fairly rustic technology, and the patternmaking is very straightforward. With iron, the shrinkage is much more of a factor. It is also easier to work lead with woodworking tools—to dress up the rough casting and to bore for bolts or plane down the mating surface.

Nonetheless, a large lead casting is still a major undertaking. The logistics of weight and heat, and also the toxicity of lead fumes and scale, all must be taken into account. They can be dealt with directly by the builder, whereas an iron casting must be done in a foundry. One advantage of iron can be that the casting has structural strength. In certain cases, this makes for a stronger hull less prone to hogging. Also, in certain cases, the less dense iron spreads the ballast mass longitudinally and vertically, giving the boat a more gentle motion and less stability.

Back to Swifty's letter:

> Let's move out on the bowsprit. As you can see from the drawing, I have put two 3-inch bronze rollers out there for the anchor and mooring lines. In the process, I have brought the whisker shrouds to the bolt that holds the chocks. This frees up the area, and you do not have to fight the whisker shrouds when working the anchor or mooring, but it still gives plenty of strength.

This is a great idea. Leave it to a builder with Swifty's experience (not only building but sailing useful cruising boats) to come up with it. Then he turned to the rig:

> I approve of the double-headsail rig, but I also have been cruising the coast of Maine when a masthead genoa is about the only way to go. There is plenty of room to pass a genoa through when tacking.
>
> If you rig both headstays with roller-furling, it would make life a lot easier. The only loss if you did this is the self-tending ability of the jibboom, and in the long run, it may not be worth it.

All along, it's been my intention to use either a roller-reefing genoa or a hanked-on genny for light air. And I agree wholeheartedly about the roller-furling. In my opinion, the self-tending jib is overrated.

Swifty then concluded:

> Nice, wide side decks and a very clear foredeck, with room for a spare anchor—yachtsman kedge, of course.
>
> Tony, it's a great boat and I do apologize if I have held you up in any way. My problem is the more I try to retire, the more I find to keep me busy. I guess I should have started to retire sooner.

Leave it to Gordon Swift to apologize for having shared his many years of practical experience with me. I understand his frustration at being so busy, but when you compare his situation with that of so many people of any age who have little or no vital interests to keep them going, I can't help but envy Swifty his fulfilling work and the health to continue with it. Perhaps this is selfish, but I wish him many more years of incomplete retirement.

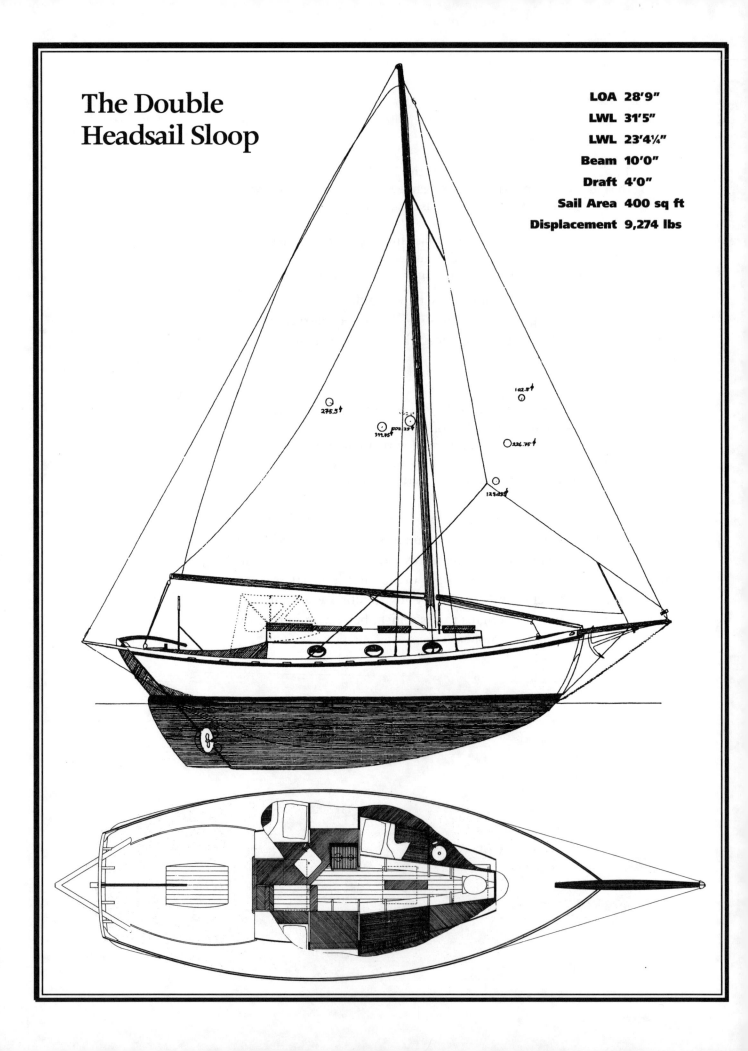

The Double
Headsail Sloop

LOA	**28'9"**
LWL	**31'5"**
LWL	**23'4¼"**
Beam	**10'0"**
Draft	**4'0"**
Sail Area	**400 sq ft**
Displacement	**9,274 lbs**

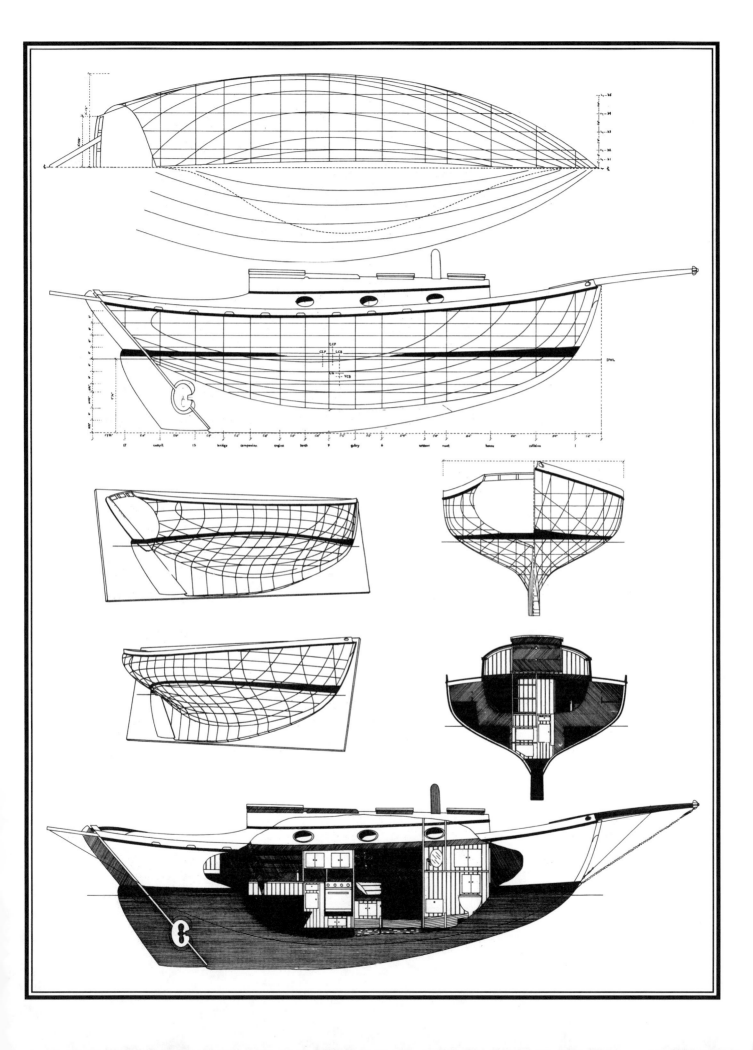

EPILOGUE

Now we've gone through the steps my clients and I have taken in the development of these eight boats—10 if we count all the tenders. No attempt has been made to "fictionalize" our interactions to make them more (or less) typical. They are what they are: my dealings with these people who are so intensely interested in boats and boat design.

What has gone on here is not a primer in "How to Design a Boat." The methods I've used and the steps we've taken reflect my particular approach with actual examples. This approach may have similarities to the way others go about designing boats, but my idiosyncrasies remove any sense of "standard practice."

At the heart of what motivates me to design boats is the desire for particularity. I want a new boat to be distinct in some way from what has come before. Even before a design sees resolution in actual construction, I want it to exhibit a unique form on paper. Thus, it doesn't come as a surprise, to me at least, that my methods—or, for that matter, the form of this book—don't conform to standard expectations.

In a world that seems to have too much of so many things—too many choices—I've always felt that I didn't want to create new designs or new boats that didn't in some way answer the question, "Why another boat?" with an affirmative declaration of their merit. I want them to say something that hasn't been said before, to excite some enthusiasm not quite articulated in the same way before, to make a connection in someone's mind and heart that hadn't been possible before. It's my fervent hope that something of the sort may be said about the pages we've just read.